ISRAEL. THE LAND
AND NATION OF DESTINY

A prophetic study of Israel, the Church
and Christendom

BY H. HAZELL SHACKCLOTH

MAY 1988
Published by
GOSPEL TRACT PUBLICATIONS
411 Hillington Road, Glasgow G52 4BL

1988
Copyright © H. Hazell Shackcloth

ISBN 0 948417 28 5

Printed by
GOSPEL TRACT PUBLICATIONS
411 Hillington Road, Glasgow. G52 4BL

Authors Quoted

Browne, Lewis: *The Story of the Jews.*
Clow, Wm., BD: *The Day of the Cross.*
Cassell's *Dictionary of Religion.*
C.I.O. Publishing: *C. of E. Response to Lima Text and ARCIC Final Report.*
Conybeare and Howson's *Life and Letters of St. Paul.*
Ellicott's Commentary (Various Contributors).
Eidersheim, Rev. D. Alfred, MA, DD: *Jesus the Messiah.*
Girdlestone, R.B., MA: *Synonyms of the O.T.*
Goodman, Geo.: *The Gospel we Preach.*
Lincoln, Wm.: *Foreshadowings in Genesis.*
Newton, Richard: *Illustrated Ramblings in Bible Lands.*
Pitt, F.W.: *The Belief that Behaves.*
Pitt, F.W.: *Coming Events Cast their Shadow Before!*
Savage, John Ashton: *The Scroll of Time.*
Scott, Walter: *Exposition of the Revelation.*
Soltau, H.W.: *The Tabernacle, its Priesthood and Offerings.*
Tatford, Dr. F.A.: *Five Minutes to Midnight.*
Trevelyan, G.M.: *Social History of England.*
Vine, W.E.: *Expository Dictionary of the N.T.*
Vine, W.E.: *The Origin and Rise of Ecclesiasticism and the Papal System.*
Young, Robert: *Analytical Concordance of the Bible.*
Young, Robert: *Concise Critical Comments.*

Acknowledgements

I wish to express my gratitude to friends who have helped and encouraged me to complete this brief volume, which has taken longer than I first intended.

My good friends Archie Hall and Dr. E.M. Applegate read the text and offered some useful comments.

The Victory Press kindly gave permission for me to use an extract from Dr. F.A. Tatford's book, *Five Minutes to Midnight*. The various other quotations are either from standard works or earlier writers, which, as far as I am aware, would now be out of copyright. If by any chance I have omitted to ask permission where it is required, I offer my apologies.

I express my appreciation to Pat Mullender and Ruth Myhill for typing the text, and the seemingly endless revisions.

Thanks are due too to Mr. A.M.S. Gooding for meticulously checking the text, and making valuable comments on doctrinal points which needed some elucidation, and in addition contributing the Foreword.

Lastly I acknowledge the debt I owe to Rachel, my wife, for her patient indulgence.

H. Hazell Shackcloth.

Outline of Typical Teaching

Foreword

'The days of the years of my pilgrimage are an hundred and thirty years, few and evil have the years of my life been, and have not attained unto the days of the years of the life of my fathers in the days of their pilgrimage.'

Comparatively, Jacob's years had been few when we consider:

Abraham 175 years (Genesis 25:7-8); Isaac 180 years (Genesis 35:28-29).

They had also been so full of evil that in desperation he could say, at the very lowest point of his chequered experience 'All these things are against me'. His later days were full of the blessing of God. He had not known, what Joseph said at a later date, 'God sent me before you to preserve you a posterity in the earth and to save your lives by a great deliverance' (Genesis 45:7).

Ere his death we read 'And when Jacob had made an end of commanding his sons, he gathered up his feet into the bed, and yielded up the ghost, and was gathered unto his people' (Genesis 49:33).

'By faith Jacob, when he was a-dying, blessed both the sons of Joseph and worshipped, leaning upon the top of his staff' (Hebrews 11:21). The Genesis record views the aged man after he had been occupied with blessing the sons of Joseph, maybe the New Testament gives us the highest account of his death—a pilgrim, his journey over, worships, leaning on the top of his staff. In spite of all the scheming, supplanting and plotting, he has reached the apex of spiritual experience—a worshipper at last!

The story of Jacob's life is full of interesting information and practical teaching for the people of God. In amongst it, however, is Jacob's notable blessing of his sons in Genesis chapter 49, full of devotional and practical truth that has been over the many years a source of encouragement, warning and instruction for the people of God. Students of the Holy Scriptures have found prophetic truth of the highest order interwoven amongst Jacob's many statements. Many authors have profitably pursued this line of investigation, holding high the lamp of prophecy. The book you are about to read approaches the subject of Jacob's sons in that way.

Mr. Hazell Shackcloth, who I first met as a boy in my 'teens, about 1930, has spent a whole life in intense study of the Word of God, and in this intriguing book gathers together a mine of wealth with regard to the nation of Israel, the distinctiveness of the Church and the morass of Christendom. The work is orthodox in doctrinal and prophetic interpretation—there are gems of truth that sparkle in its pages. I, personally, am indebted to the author for the information I have gleaned as I have perused the manuscript. It contains an illuminating section on Ecumenical Error that will be helpful and interesting to all who have discerning minds.

This is a book that all the saints should read.

A.M. Salway Gooding.

Introduction

'Now these things occurred as examples'
(1 Corinthians 10:6 N.I.V)

What the seed or nursery-bed is to the gardener, and the entrance hall of a great house to the architect, so the book of Genesis is, and much more, to the one who reads and reveres God's Word. It not merely serves as an introduction to the Book, but is an integral part of the whole.

We owe it to this book to enlighten us as to the Divine nature, as various titles are given to the Godhead when some new facet of His character, or some attribute, is first revealed to man.

The same book tells us all that can be known for certain about the creation, or the Fall of Man, about God's holy judgments tempered with His mercy, and of the origins of the nations and their manifold languages.

But what also gives it special distinction is the record of its rich characters as they make their marks on the pages of history. These people are the embodiment of great truths in themselves. We call them *types* for convenience since they illustrate important principles which are formulated throughout the Book. We use the word *illustrate* advisedly, the essential doctrines are the real subject matter of the Bible. The stories may be used at different times, even by the same people in diverse ways, but if such usage throws light on some fundamental truth the method is thereby justified. It is with this view that we take up the story of the births of the twelve sons of Jacob, who not only became the foundation members of the nation of Israel, but, as their names suggest, much more beside, as we hope to demonstrate.

From the days of Abraham, Jacob's grandfather, the principle of faith in God was common to the three generations concerned including Jacob himself. This was to be the hall-mark for all time of those who find favour with God. Even as it was said of Abraham, 'he believed God and it was counted unto him for righteousness' Galatians 3:6. This is not to say that these were perfect men; the record of their lives proves otherwise, but they honoured God by declaring that He was worthy of their trust. Faith in God is not the prerogative of man in any one age, therefore in the story of these births and certain events in their lives we are privileged to have a brief glimpse of truths fully developed in other Scriptures.

The chart preceding this introduction is intended to give a 'bird's eye' view of the subject to enable the reader to follow the sequence of events, as the manner of the births of Jacob's sons, and the striking meanings of their names, are seen to form a prophetic picture.

It will be noted that the subject of surrogation plays a prominent part in the story of Jacob, and we interpret this as something utterly displeasing to God. As it is frequently in the news at the time of writing, the warnings implicit in the story should be heeded by all who under-estimate this form of adultery. Jacob's two wives, Rachel and Leah, were not without an example of its baneful consequences since Sarah, Abram's wife, when herself barren, had offered her handmaid, Hagar, for a like purpose. She lived to regret her action, saying, 'My wrong *be* upon thee; I have given my maid into thy bosom; and when she had conceived, I was despised in her eyes; the Lord judge between me and thee' (Genesis 16:5).

What is here presented is in broad agreement with the views of accredited prophetic students of the past, such as Walter Scott, and A.C. Gaebelein and many others. The writer cannot lay claim to such scholarship, but has the advantage of more recent history which in a few cases has called for slight modifications of their conclusions about minor details.

Our treatment of the origins of the sons of Jacob, is the first of three statements concerning them in the Pentateuch. The second was by Jacob himself, who prophesied of the tribes as he was dying, and faithfully depicted their strengths and weaknesses, one by one (Genesis 49).

The only period into which this prediction can be fitted, corresponds with their occupation of Canaan from the time of Joshua.

The third prophecy was made by Moses at the end of his life (Deuteronomy 33). And by contrast makes no mention of Israel's failures. It therefore, anticipates the period of Israel's restoration and blessing under her Messiah in the Millennial Kingdom, as verses 28-29 indicate.

Our approach will be seen to demonstrate how men of faith bring blessings to mankind which transcend dispensational conditions.

The blessings stemming from the faith of such men as Abraham and Jacob reach out to ourselves and to a future which is, even now, the subject of prophecy.

It may be objected that any representation of the people of God, could not admit of two brides existing side by side. Such an argument might well be presented by those who no longer hold the view that God's purposes take account of both an earthly and an heavenly people, rather that Israel is spiritually represented in the church with no distinct prophetic future. No such objections will be raised on the part of those who firmly believe, on scriptural authority, that Israel will again be restored to favour at a future time, and will finally occupy 'the new earth', as stated in the book of Revelation (chapter 21).

The church by contrast is described as an heavenly people, who will inhabit the new heaven but nevertheless will have a distinctive role in the Millennial kingdom.

An earlier writer has disposed of the imagined problem of the two brides in these words.

'To the fact of the two brides of the Lord, the heavenly and the earthly, the objection has been made that 'then one would be for the parlour and the other for the hall'.

The answer is, 'in that day, heaven and earth will be so full of the glory, that neither sphere will resemble 'the hall'.

That the glory of the celestial should differ from and excel the glory of the terrestrial is no wonder, and the type of Asenath the 'bride' of the ruler at the end of Genesis with his brethren at his feet prove that where the heavenly and the earthly are both represented, the heavenly one is the bride.'

Foreshadowings in Genesis by William Lincoln p.117.

When considering the two women a distinction needs to be made between Israel, Jehovah's earthly wife and the church, the bride of Christ, the Lamb's wife.

The former has been set aside for the period of the churches' witness because of unbelief, when as Jeremiah prophesied:

'Surely as a wife treacherously departed from her husband, so have ye dealt treacherously with me O house of Israel, saith the Lord' (*Jehovah Adonai*) (Jeremiah 3:20).

Soon the apostate church will suffer a similar fate following the coming of the Lord for His bride the true church (Romans 11:21-22, 24).

Finally, Israel will once more return to God's favour as the nation acknowledges Christ as its Messiah, whom it once rejected (Romans 11:25-29, Zechariah 13:6-9).

The reader will have no difficulty in accepting that Rachel was first and foremost in the affections of Jacob. That Leah was 'hated' may present some initial difficulty.

This may be resolved by a comparison of three statements:—

(1) 'And Jacob loved Rachel' (Genesis 29:18).

(2) 'He loved Rachel also more than Leah' (v.30).

(3) The Lord saw that Leah was hated (v.31).

These terms 'love' and 'hatred' serve to illustrate a special feature in Hebrew writing, which in some circumstances lacks the shades of meaning, familiar to Western cultures, in describing extreme emotions.

Dr. Young, the compiler of the Concordance which bears his name in No. 39 of the 'Hints and Helps to Bible Interpretation' makes this comment:—

'The verb 'to hate' is frequently used for 'to love less' (as Genesis 29:30 (2) above) See Genesis 29:31; Deuteronomy 21:15; Malachi 1:3 (and several New Testament passages quoted).

This observation may well explain many other seemingly extreme statements in scripture which need to be compared with the entire body of revealed truth, dealing with the subject in view at the time. As Peter's epistle states 'no prophecy of scripture is of any private interpretation' (2 Peter 1:20).

'The writers of scripture did not put *their own* interpretation upon the God-breathed words they wrote' (Vine).

The circumstances relating to Jacob's wives is codified among the sundry laws of the Book of Deuteronomy, and throws much light on the typical teaching concerning the first four sons of Leah. We quote in full:—

'If a man have two wives, one beloved,

and another hated, and they have born him children, both the beloved and the hated; and if the first-born son be hers that was hated; then it shall be, when he maketh his sons to inherit that which he hath, that he may not make the son of the beloved first-born before the son of the hated, which is indeed the first-born. But he shall acknowledge the son of the hated for the first-born, by giving him a *double portion* of all that he hath: for he is the beginning of his strength; the right of the first-born is his' (Deuteronomy 21:15-17).

The salient features of this arrangement would ensure that the four first sons of Leah would inherit special advantages from the family depositions when the inheritance came to be shared out.

Reuben would have prior claim to his father's inheritance as *'the beginning of his strength'* (v.17), a phrase used by Jacob in the course of his prophecy of the twelve tribes in future Canaan conditions in the 'last days', following the wilderness wanderings (Genesis 49:3). His particular blessing would be the privileges of the firstborn (which his father Jacob had obtained by deception but which none the less would pass to him as of right (Deuteronomy 21:16).

This entitled him to a *Double-Portion* of the inheritance (v.17) of the family and tribe. The *Double-Portion* is frequently referred to as a symbol of divine favour and blessing.

Isaiah (ch.61) was partly fulfilled, as our Lord confirmed, in the synagogue at Nazareth (Luke 4:21). As He spake of the blessings to be enjoyed by those who saw His first coming as 'the acceptable year of the Lord' (v.19), and who became His followers. But the complete fulfilment will be in Isaiah's words:— 'Therefore *in their land* they shall possess *the Double'* (Isaiah 61:7).

All is to be to the *praise of His glory* (Ephesians 1:12,14). And what is more, the church on earth has a *Double Portion* too, for, 'godliness is profitable unto all things, having promise for the life *that now is* and *of that which* is *to come'* (1 Timothy 4:8); we can say with the Psalmist, 'Blessed is the man whose transgression is forgiven, whose sin is covered" (Psalm 32:1).

The Authorised Version's interpretation of Jacob's sons' names, as they were given at the time of birth have been used for this work. It is the only example we have in all the Scriptures where every member of a large family has been given a significant name at birth. It is such exceptions in the inspired Word which sometimes give a pointer to some important truth.

The Hebrew people had a proclivity toward attaching distinctive names to their offspring; occasionally, as in this instance, with what we regard as some prophetic message and at other times with an allusion to passing circumstances. There have been instances regretably, where interpretations of names have been forced at the expense of truth. Our purpose has been to use them as pointers to the solutions of many present day problems which can be found only in the complete body of the Divine revelations, the Scriptures.

Rachel — the Deposed Wife

'because of unbelief they were broken off'
(Romans 11:20).

Before considering the individual births of the sons of Jacob we need to discover the reasons for the setting aside of Rachel, the bride first promised to the patriarch, since these have a distinct bearing on the typical teaching which relates to Israel and the church.

From the very brief descriptions which are given of the two girls, we are bound to conclude that Rachel had a more attractive disposition than her sister Leah. Her spontaneous welcome given to Jacob as he first met her at Sychar's well must have deeply impressed him. We may well understand how that Laban wishing to please the couple concerned would agree, with mental reservations, to terms by which Jacob could marry Rachel, since there was an impediment according to tradition which would have denied her the right to marry before the older sister, Leah.

In this we have an instance of man's proposals and God's disposals. On the anointing of David to the high office of kingship in Israel we have another such example; one by one the sons of Jesse appeared before the prophet Samuel, each one it seemed adequately met all the requirements, only to be rejected as the Lord said unto Samuel, 'Look not on his countenance, or on the height of his stature; because I have refused him: for *the Lord seeth* not as man seeth; for man looketh on the outward appearance, but the Lord looketh on the heart' (1 Samuel 16:7).

There are many more telling reasons given us for the setting aside of Rachel than of Jesse's sons. It can be seen from the story as it unfolds, that having been brought up in a house where idolatry was practised, she must have condoned the practice even to the extent of stealing her father's idols, and secreting them in her camel's furniture; and further, preventing their discovery when Laban had caught up with the company after their surreptitious departure. She thus compounded her offence by a specious falsehood (Genesis 31:30-32). In addition to this we see her readiness to take the initiative in offering her handmaid to Jacob in concubinage in an attempt to frustrate the purposes of God (Genesis 30:1-6).

Regarding Rachel as a type of Israel after the flesh, she accurately illustrates God's reasons for setting the nation aside in favour of the predominately Gentile church set forth by Leah.

The relationship of Israel with her neighbours in the pagan world, and her willingness to follow their idolatrous practices are related so frequently, in the history of the nation, that one hardly needs to point out any single act of sacrilege. It seems to be a principle of revelation that where sin is inherent it is soon made apparent to all. This is seen in the

Genesis account of the fall, as sin's harvest is reproduced immediately in the lives of the first children both of Adam and his rebellious son, Cain. Similarly idolatry, Israel's most grievous sin, had fully borne fruit even before Moses had opportunity to present the law, which forbade idolatry, while Aaron complied with the demands of the people to make them a visible ELOHIM to worship after the manner of their pagan neighbours.

Israel should have been as aware, as was Abram when he left Ur, that God would brook no rivalry with the false ELOHIM of the pagan world. As R.B. Girdlestone rightly says:— 'The primary lesson the Lord sought to teach was that they were to restore the name ELOHIM to its original sole owner. 'Thou shalt have no other ELOHIM before Me'. *Synonyms of the Old Testament* p.21. Equally emphatic are the statements of Exodus 23:13 and 2 Kings 19:18, each of which names the rival false gods as ELOHIM.

Bearing in mind the unrewarding witness of the prophets as they laboured faithfully in their endeavours to restore to Israel the true worship of Jehovah, we can see how readily the people of God can be influenced by paganism. Painstaking researchers such as Hislop, have traced the pagan worship of both ancient and modern times to Nimrod, a descendant of Cain, the founder of Babylon. The worship of Ashteroth and Baal with many other pagan deities have also been traced to this source. The former is named no less than nine times in the Old Testament, on the occasions when Israel practised pagan worship.

F.W. Pitt too included a chapter entitled 'Mystery Babylon' in his book, *'Coming Events Cast their Shadows Before'* a useful guide, well detailed, for those who may have access to this 'out of print' title. Even allowing for the possibility of some degree of legend in this line of study, it cannot be denied that much of the paganism which has been embodied in the liturgy of the historic churches of Christendom can be traced to this source. Christians who desire to worship and serve the Lord according to the pattern outlined in the New Testament must guard against any introduction of such practices, meanwhile ensuring that man-made rules and prejudices contrary to the Word are not to become a substitute for such errors.

In spite of the severance of Israel during the present dispensation, we must never lose sight of God's covenant promises made to Abraham, concerning his seed which will be made good at a time which accords with His will.

The patience of God with Israel in the past is a continual reminder to us of His long forbearance with His people in every other age, and of His inflexible holiness when once apostasy develops beyond the point of His endurance. At the time of witness of the prophets and again during our Lord's ministry, Israel was warned of judgment as the only alternative to apostasy. This, in turn, was succeeded by the witness of the apostles until it reached the point where Paul was compelled to turn from them with the words, 'It was necessary that the word of God should first have been spoken to you; but seeing ye put it from you, and judge yourselves unworthy of ever-lasting life, lo we turn to the Gentiles' (Acts 13:46).

The need for our awareness of the love of Christ to His church, is expressed in Paul's prayer, 'That Christ may dwell in your hearts by faith; that ye being rooted and grounded in love, may be able to comprehend with all saints what is the breadth, and length, and depth, and height; and to know the love of Christ, which passeth knowledge!' (Ephesians 3:17-19).

The comparative love of Christ to Israel and to the church is aptly stated by Mr William Lincoln as follows, 'Never did Israel in her palmiest days of yore: never will she; never can she, in any such day to come, hear language from the Lord commensurate with this, 'As my father hath loved me so have I loved you' and, 'Thou hast loved them as thou hast loved me'.

Those united to Christ by faith may take comfort from the fact that as members of the true church they are represented by Leah rather than Rachel, and privileged to have their part in the dispensation of the grace of God, alongside those who 'turned to God from idols to serve the living and true God; and to wait for His Son from heaven (1 Thessalonians 1:9-10).

How fitting is the apostle's description of this strange turn of events as he quotes from Hosea, 'I will call them my people which were not my people (Lo Ammi) and her beloved which was not beloved. And it shall come to pass, that in the place where it was said to them, Ye are not my people there shall they be called the children of the living God' (Hosea 2:23; Romans 9:25-6).

Having previously traced the cause of the fall of Israel to its idolatry, after centuries of warnings from God through the prophets there is no real disparity between Paul's diagnosis of Israel's ills and that of the said prophets; idolatry and *unbelief* go hand in hand, and unbelief is seen to result in unrighteousness as Paul quotes from Isaiah 28:16, 'Behold I lay in Sion a stumblingstone and rock of offence: and whosoever *believeth* on Him shall not be ashamed' (Romans 9:33).

As to righteousness he wrote '*they sought it* not by faith, but, as it were by the works of the law' (Romans 9:32).

At such a time as this the church may well be reminded of its need for practical righteousness; the parenthetical chapters (9-11 Romans) warn us that what has happened for our blessing by default, can be, and one day will be, reversed, as a result of the apostasy of Christendom, for 'There shall come out of Sion the Deliverer, and shall turn away ungodliness from Jacob' (Isaiah 59:20 and Romans 11:26).

The union of Jacob and Leah was not only unexpected by both parties, but soon proved fruitful, as did the church in its early days: especially when we consider that for many centuries God had extended His long suffering patience with Israel, but to no purpose in the end. The Shekinah glory, the most impressive symbol of God's presence, had departed from the Temple in Ezekiel's day, and any meaningful worship of God in Old

Testament terms had become casuistic and dead, as the old order dragged on; only to be replaced by this new movement from God which proved fruitful in its results from the very beginning, as many turned to the Lord.

3

Reuben: See a Son

'Beloved, now are we the sons of God' (1 John 3:2).

The birth of Reuben, Jacob's first son, is an example of God's overruling in face of human opposition. The patriarch's undeviating choice of a bride had settled on Rachel, but this had been thwarted by Laban's intrigue, and proved in the end to have been in the line of the Divine will, by the fruitfulness of Jacob's union with Leah instead.

Reuben's birth followed an extended history of persecution which Leah suffered at Rachel's hands, because of her deep seated jealousy. The event called forth Leah's joyful response, 'See a son'; but her delight was tinged with the memory of the affliction she had endured as she remarked, 'Surely the LORD has looked upon my affliction, now therefore my husband will love me' (Genesis 29:32).

As we consider Reuben's birth it may serve a useful purpose to be reminded at the outset that the blessings of our sonship* in God's family were possible only at the expense of the Saviour's afflictions on the Cross. As Frazer's hymn reflects,

---

*We use the term 'sons' in the generic sense, representing both sexes, as a scriptural precedent.

'Tis there thy grace unbounded,
And perfect love we see;
With joy and yet *with sorrow*
We do remember Thee.'

Isaiah saw it all in his vision, saying, 'In all their
afflictions, He was afflicted', and again, 'Surely He
hath borne our griefs and carried our sorrows: yet
we did esteem Him stricken, smitten of God and
afflicted' (Isaiah 63:9; 53:4 Newberry).

Paul too could count it joy to share in part in these
sufferings with the believers in the early church
and say:

'I...rejoice in my sufferings for you, and fill up
that which is behind of the afflictions of Christ
in my flesh for His body's sake, which is the
church' (Colossians 1:23-24).

As to the words 'fill up' Lightfoot remarks:

'That Christ the sinless Master should
have left something for Paul the unworthy
servant to suffer: and in so doing expresses
the truth that Christ in the first instance
knew the depths of not only humanly
imposed suffering, but was stricken smitten and afflicted of God.'

The subject of sonship as seen in Reuben's birth
may seem remote until we relate it as a type to the
entire range of revealed truth of Scripture concerning Israel and the Church.

Not for the first time in the history of the fathers
was a son born in unusual circumstances. Abram's
first son Ishmael was denied the recognition
accorded to a firstborn son by Hebrew tradition,
being the son of an handmaid. Later in life when the

natural processes of birth would preclude any hope of progeny, a 'son of promise' was born to the aged parents. Isaac's birth by a parent who considered herself to be sterile with age provides more than a hint that he foreshadowed One who, even to a greater degree was born contrary to the laws of nature (Isaiah 9:6). If we relate this fact to his enacted death on Moriah's mount, and also note the conditions which were imposed upon Eliezer, Abraham's servant as he set forth to procure a bride for Isaac (Genesis 24:7), we are presented with a striking picture of the Divine Sonship.

Beyond the need for a son to be born to promote the national hopes of Israel through the Abrahamic line, these circumstances in Israel's life foreshadow that other Son, the Son of God Himself (Galatians 4:4).

> 'Jesus who was made a little lower than the angels for the suffering of death crowned with glory and honour, that He by the grace of God should taste death for every man. For it became him for whom are all things, and by whom are all things, *in bringing many sons unto glory*, to make the captain of their salvation perfect through suffering. For He that sanctifieth and they who are sanctified are all of one (Father): for which cause He is not ashamed to call them brethren' (Hebrews 2:9-11).

In this the Lord and His people have a common Father, and it is to His sons we now turn our attention.

II

The idea of God having a sonship vested in a people is first stated at the time immediately before the Exodus, when Israel was delivered from its bondage in Egypt. Moses was directed to say to Pharoah:

'Thus saith the Lord, Israel *is* my son, even my firstborn: And I say unto thee, Let my son go that he may serve me, and if thou refuse to let him go, behold, I will slay thy son, even thy first born.' (Exodus 4:22-23).

This relationship was acknowledged by God over many centuries of patient forbearance until even at the end of Old Testament times when Israel, by then out of favour, was promised once more to be restored to its intended relationship with God, as it is said, 'In that day when I make up my jewels; I will spare them as a man spareth his own son that serveth him' (Malachi 3:17).

With Rachel suffering a temporary set-back, Leah on the other hand is seen to be in the ascendancy as she rejoices in the birth of her firstborn son, as it is recorded, 'She bare a son, and she called his name Reuben' (Margin: See a son) (Genesis 29:32). In Christian terms sonship is enjoyed to a far deeper degree than Israel ever knew; in this Rachel truly represents Israel.

John, the disciple and apostle, with the insight

which is a feature of his writings, gives priority to the sonship of believers in the prologue of his Gospel, after noting Israel's rejection of the option, by saying, 'to as many as received Him, to them gave He the power (right or privilege) to become the *Sons of God*' (John 1:12). Therefore, since all share in the depravity of man, it is fitting that salvation and fatherhood be offered to all without distinction, or as another wrote, 'God hath concluded them all in unbelief, that he might have mercy upon all' (Romans 11:32).

Later, John must have deeply felt the wonder of this new relationship, enjoyed only by faith, as he exclaimed,

> 'How great is the love the Father has
> lavished on us, that we should be called
> children of God! and that is what we are!'
> (1 John 3:1 NIV).

As a man who had once been described as one of the 'Sons of thunder', the realisation must have overwhelmed him. By what means this unique relationship is brought about is given high priority in the New Testament teaching and deserves our fullest consideration.

It is quite clear from the Saviour's conversation with Nicodemus (John 3), for example, that sonship, which the Jewish reader could understand as a physical process only, is, spiritually only possible by a person being 'born again', by faith in Christ and His atoning death (see note below). As the highest authority He could say with a word of caution, 'Except a man be born again, (from above) he cannot see the kingdom of God (v.3); (see 1 Peter

1:23-25). Would that those who lead people into the interminable maze of comparative religion might consider the indisputable claim of Christ, 'I am the way, the truth, and the life; no man cometh unto the Father, but by Me' (John 14:6).

There are three terms used to describe the incidence of the new birth in John's Gospel (apart from descriptions elsewhere such as 'receiving Him', 'believing on His name', and being 'born again', all of which are synonymous phrases, and each assuming trust in, and a committal to, the Lordship of Christ (John 3:14-16 and 1:12). A mere mental assent is insufficient; a revolutionary change of life in the form of discipleship and nothing less is called for of every son.*

An expression used by Paul, 'Having predestinated us unto the adoption of children by Jesus Christ to himself' (Ephesians 1:5) might lead one to assume

---

*Note: It is regrettable that some American politicians have sought to advance their prospects by calling themselves 'born again Christians'. Their commitment is to be subjects, not rulers, as those who pay, pray for, and obey the government of the day, without disobeying the Word (Romans 13:1-7).

A politically motivated power seeking church becomes a corrupt church as was the case in Tudor England, as G M Trevelyan writes:

> 'Cardinal Wolsey displayed on a colossal scale the pride and pawn of the medieval church, himself the instrument of Papal power...He treated the lay nobles and gentlemen like dirt beneath his feet, thereby helping to prepare the anti-clerical revolution that accompanied his fall. He kept a household of nearly a thousand persons and marched in state with silver pillars and pole-axes borne before him.' *English Social History* (page 94).

that more than one way is open to us to become sons in God's family. Although the word 'adoption' has more than one connotation (as in its reference to Israel, Romans 9:4) its meaning is always 'placing as a son', the idea conveyed by the phrase being, 'placed in a position suited to his status'. W E Vine's comment on this verse is as follows:

> 'They (children) are said to have been foreordained unto adoption of sons through Jesus Christ (RV). The AV 'adoption of children' is a mistranslation and misleading. God does not adopt believers as children; they are begotten as such by the Holy Spirit through faith. Adoption is a term involving the dignity of the relationship of the believers as sons; it is not a putting in to the *family* by spiritual birth, but a putting into the *position* of sons'.
>
> *Dictionary of New Testament Words* p.24.

The subject of predestination in the above named text would seem to refer to such matters as Christian service and is only used for example in the case of the Apostle Paul after conversion (Acts 26:15-18). The unconverted person should not be confused by the word. His eternal interest rests in obedience to the call of God in the Gospel. After that what he has been fitted for will be revealed. It is in the enjoyment of this intimate relationship that the believer is not regarded as a servant (i.e. a bond-slave) with its attendant fears, but a free-born son who counts it a privilege to serve! Paul described

Timothy, one of his spiritual progeny — 'as a son with the father he served with me in the gospel' (Philippians 2:22). This freedom to serve was illustrated by Stephen at his martyrdom, quoting God's statement at the time of the Exodus, 'That nation to whom they shall be *in bondage* will I judge, and after that they shall come forth and serve me in this place' (Acts 7:7). Theirs was to be a service of freedom even as the Apostle Paul wrote, 'you did not receive a spirit which makes you a slave again to fear, but you received the Spirit of sonship. And by Him we cry, Abba, Father' (Romans 8:15 NIV). The blessings of the gospel not only ensure that the believer shares with the Son, a Father, not on the basis of Deity but of grace, but also an inheritance on the same basis. It, by far, transcends anything promised to Israel in the coming Millennial day, attractive as it will surely be. The details given of it are but few, but tell us that unlike the 'corn and wine' of that day, 'they which are called...receive the promise of an eternal inheritance' (Hebrews 9:15); 'sealed with that holy Spirit of promise, which is the earnest of our inheritance until the redemption of the purchased possession, unto the praise of his glory' (Ephesians 1:13-14); and *since you are a son*, God has made you also an heir' (Galatians 4:7 NIV) and the inheritance is 'incorruptible and undefiled and fadeth not away, reserved in heaven (1 Peter 1:4). The Christian's prospect is manifestly not bound up with the tawdry things of earth, but 'the things which are not seen, *the* eternal' (2 Corinthians 4:18).

Yet another descriptive title of God's sons is

'Sons of light'. The Lord gave them this name on the first day of the fateful week of His crucifixion. It began in an atmosphere of euphoria as the excited crowd hailed Him as their coming Messiah, with the prophetic quotation, 'Blessed is the King of Israel that cometh in the name of the Lord' (John 12:13; Psalm 118:26). This vapid enthusiasm was to give place within five short days to the cry, 'Away with *him*, crucify him' (John 19:18); so readily could the vacillating crowd be stirred from receiving Him to rejecting Him! Even the disciples had forgotten these familiar words until after Christ's resurrection and at the last deserted Him in His hour of need, when their presence would have been welcome as never before! The Pharisees' response was predictable as they witnessed the procession with its palm leaves 'strawed in the way'. 'Perceive', they said, 'how ye prevail nothing? Behold the world is gone after him' (John 12:19); a premature observation which had taken little account of the fickleness of mob behaviour! It was on this day as the impending darkness of the Cross drew ever nearer that He used an expression once spoken to Nicodemus (John 3) 'and I, if I *be lifted up from the earth*, I will draw all men unto me' (John 12:32). This allusion to the Cross seemed to the people a denial of His earlier Messianic claims. Their time of opportunity was passing with but five days to run their course as He cautioned them, 'Yet a little while is the light with you ... while ye have light believe in the light, that ye may be *children* (*Sons* NIV) of light. These things spake Jesus and departed from them and did hide himself from them' (John 12:32-36). Their day had ended as suddenly as it will for the people of our day when the Master rises up to 'shut to the door' (Luke 13:25).

As in creation's day, the Christian is the 'lesser light' as he reflects the glory of 'the Sun of Righteousness'. 'For God who commanded the light to shine out of darkness, hath shined in our hearts, to *give* the light of the glory of God in the face of Jesus Christ' (2 Corinthians 4:6). If our witness is in some small degree effective it entirely redounds to God's glory since 'we have this treasure in earthen vessels, that the excellency of the power may be of God, and not of us' (v.7).

The figure is of 'jars of clay' which in ancient times were used as receptacles for a monarch's treasures. Paul could write elsewhere, 'Unto me, who am *less than the least of all saints* is this grace given, that I should preach among the Gentiles the unsearchable riches of Christ' (Ephesians 3:8). We are to be as 'sons of God, without rebuke in the midst of a crooked and perverse nation, among whom ye shine, as lights in the world' (Philippians 2:15).

This simile has a practical application, alas, too often ignored, and our directive is this, 'Ye were sometimes darkness but now *are ye* light in the Lord: walk as children of light' (Ephesians 5:8). The men of faith of Hebrews 11 were formed of the common clay of humanity, but 'out of weakness were made strong' (v.34). May we seek to follow their example and 'run with patience the race that is set before us' (Hebrews 12:1).

The life of faith is never to be considered a 'soft

option' by which we may escape the rigours of life, rather, it calls for discipline as the Hebrew believers were warned, 'My son, despise not thou the chastening (lit. child training) of the Lord, nor faint when thou art rebuked of Him: For whom the Lord loveth He chasteneth, and scourgeth *every son* whom He receiveth' (Hebrews 12:5-6). It is the final result that counts!

Lastly, it is essential for the sons of God to realise that their citizenship (politics) is in heaven (Philippians 3:20). In His last prayer our Lord said, 'They are not of the world, even as I am not of the world' (John 17:16). The 'world' in this context means 'the present condition of human affairs in alienation from and opposition to God' (Vine). The Corinthian epistle makes it abundantly clear that the Christian and the world cannot possibly have any common ground, as Paul writes:

"Be ye not unequally yoked together with unbelievers: for what fellowship hath righteousness with unrighteousness? and what communion hath light with darkness? And what concord hath Christ with Belial? or what part hath he that believeth with an infidel? And what agreement hath the temple of God with idols? for ye are the temple of the living God: as God hath said, I will dwell in them, and walk in *them*; and I will be their God, and they shall be my people. Wherefore come out from among them, and be ye separate, saith the Lord, and touch not the unclean *thing*; and I will receive you, and *will be a Father unto*

you, and ye shall be my sons and daughters, saith
the Lord Almighty" (2 Corinthians
6:14-18).

The first half of this passage (vs.14-16a) is
Pauline in its origin, and the second half (vs.16b-18)
from 'as God hath said' is evidently taken from the
Old Testament, and seems to have caused translators
some difficulty in deciding its source. The Authorised
Version, Good News and New International Versions
together quote from 14 different texts, and only
two of them agree with one other version. It is far
more likely that Paul quoted from one passage only,
i.e. Ezekiel ch. 14, which none of the three included
among its references.

The following comparison will demonstrate the
agreement to be seen between the Old Testament
passage as it related to Israel, and similar principles
which are vitally important when applied to the
Church.

(a) Israel was practising the idolatry of its
pagan neighbours (Ezekiel 14:6-7).
Paul details the incompatibility between Christian
standards, and those that emanate from Belial,
including idolatry (2 Corinthians 6:14-16a).

(b) Israel is reminded of God's oft repeated
statement 'that they may be my people,
and I may be their God' (v.11).
Paul says 'what agreement hath the temple of
God with idols? for ye are the temple of the living
God, as God hath said, I will dwell in them, and I will
be their God and they shall be my people' (v.16).

(c) The prophet cites the examples of
three truly separated men, namely, Noah,

Job and Daniel* (vs 14, 16, 18, 20) who in spite of their godly walk, 'could not *deliver son nor daughter*' (v.20).

Paul writes, 'Wherefore come out from among them, and be ye separate, saith the Lord, and touch not the unclean *thing*, and I will receive you' (v.17).

(d) Looking forward to the time of Israel's restoration in the Messianic Kingdom the prophet says, 'I will send my four judgments upon Jerusalem ... Yet behold therein shall be left a remnant that shall be brought forth, both *sons and daughters* ... and they shall comfort you when ye see their ways and their doings' (vs.21-23 abbrev.).

Paul concludes: 'I will be a Father unto you, and ye shall be my *sons and daughters*, saith the Lord Almighty' (v.18).

This is the only instance when Paul addresses the mixed company of believers as 'sons and daughters'. His normal practice is to refer to them as 'brethren' (Romans 12:1 etc.) or 'Holy brethren' (Hebrews 3:1), the female members being seen as part of 'mankind' and 'of the man' as expressed by Paul (1 Corinthians 11:8).

In making this distinction, Paul would teach us that in the exercise of the activities of the church, differing as they do in character by both men and women, each must see to it that the principle of separation is strictly observed to avoid any division

---

*Daniel was a contemporary of Ezekiel, at least in his early life (Daniel 1 and 2).

in the Church, or a grieving of the Spirit to the detriment of all. This applies not only to the work of the local church, but extends to dress, deportment, duties and headship, all of which are clearly defined in the New Testament epistles.

4

Simeon — 'Heard'

GOD'S HOUSE OF PRAYER

'Praying always with all prayer and supplication in the Spirit' (Ephesians 6:18).

The thought which must have been uppermost in the mind of Leah, as she gave birth to her second son is made clear by her comment, 'The Lord hath *heard* that I was hated, and hath given me this son also: and she called his name Simeon' (Heb. 'Heard') (Genesis 29:33).

It would be an unthinkable situation if the children of God had no means of communication with the Father of the family! In such a case they would fare worse than the family of the unbeliever. But the truth is far better, for we have the Spirit's assurance by the hand of Paul that, 'God hath sent forth the Spirit of His Son into your hearts, crying, Abba, Father' (Galatians 4:6).

The example of Leah suggests two ways in which we may engage in prayer; firstly, as supplicants in times of stress; and secondly, as grateful beneficiaries when the Lord's response is seen to have been made. There are, of course, other ways of savouring the sense of communion with God, as by interceding on behalf of others, and in the community of the church, by corporate worship. But as these profound subjects deserve more than a passing mention, we must confine ourselves to those aspects of prayer which are suggested by Leah's trying circumstances.

In her grief it would have been an understandable human response if Leah's prayer had been imprecatory, since she had more than sufficient time to reflect on its cause, namely, her own sister's jealousy, but it must be admitted that her father Laban was not without fault in the matter, and it is evident that vindictiveness played no part in Leah's temperament; rather her prayer was an intreaty that a means of consolation might be found for her in her sorry situation, as indeed happened.

It was considered to be a sign of God's favour and blessing among Hebrew women to bear children; barrenness was deemed to be a grievous affliction, for as the book of Psalms has it 'Happy *is* the man that hath his quiver full of them' (Psalm 127:5). In their reactions to their respective situations the two women in this story conform to a familiar pattern as to the causes and consequences of jealousy.

It may be said that every prayer has to comply with two essential conditions. Firstly, it must concur with the sovereign will of God, and secondly, also accept that there is a precise time for its answer, known only to the Lord. His Divine attributes require these essential provisions. A few examples may be adduced which will serve to show that the answer may be withheld for many long years, where the far-seeing mind of God is concerned with the destinies of men and nations. Leah's waiting time of no more than two or three years, would be brief by comparison, and the second birth confirmed the mind of God by its double witness, to the fulfilment of His ultimate purposes.

The most remarkable example of unanswered prayer is seen in the awaited fulfilment of the Messianic hope of Israel. This was implied in God's promises to Abraham, and has been often referred to specifically since Jacob prophesied that, 'The sceptre shall not depart from Judah, nor a lawgiver from between his feet, until Shiloh come: and unto him shall the gathering of the people be' (Genesis 49:10).

Balaam too, the man hired by Balak the King of the Moabites to curse the people of Israel, could do no other than bless them with the prophecy, 'Out of Jacob shall come he that shall have dominion' (Numbers 24:19).

To this day the orthodox Jews go to the Wailing Wall of the Temple ruins, especially on a Friday, to pray for the coming and rule of their Messiah, and meanwhile read and make responses to the Old Testament Scriptures, little realising that the One they rejected and crucified will be the long promised Messiah (Zechariah 13:6).

Closely associated with the hope of Israel is that of the church as she awaits the Coming Again of Christ, which will be the first phase of future prophetic fulfilment. The realisation of this 'blessed hope' as it is termed, has been the subject of the prayers of believers since it was promised the disciples by the Lord Himself (John 14:3). The very last prayer of the New Testament is the subject of it, 'He that testifieth these things saith, 'Surely, I come quickly. Amen. *Even so come, Lord Jesus'* (Revelation 22:20).

In spite of the long waiting time before the fulfilment of these prophecies, the end is certain, for, 'Yet a little while and he that shall come will come, and will not tarry' (Hebrews 10:37), or as Mr Vine renders it, 'a little while, how little, how little'!

These events will each take place precisely at the predetermined moment, as the Lord said to His disciples, 'But of that day and hour knoweth no man, no, not the angels of heaven, but my Father only' (Matthew 24:36).

Later at the time of His ascension, in answer to the disciples enquiry as to the possibility of an early fulfilment of the long awaited Messianic promise Christ told them, 'It is not for you to know the times or the seasons, which the Father hath put in His own power' (Acts 1:7). We can come to but one conclusion as we witness the foreboding 'signs of the times' both in the world at large and the church too, with no risk of presumption on our part that 'the coming of the Lord draweth nigh' (James 5:8). Scoffers may ask, 'Where are the signs of His coming?' but the people immediately concerned in that day, the godly remnant of Israel, will heed the Lord's words, 'when these things begin to come to pass, then look up, and lift up your heads; for your redemption draweth nigh' (Luke 21:28).

Another event in ancient times which, for long, awaited God's promises was the ending of the captivity of the Israelites in Egypt, at the time of the Exodus. In this God fulfilled two of His predictions. The length of their sojourn was to be four hundred and thirty years from the time of God's covenant with Abraham (Exodus 12:40; Galatians 3:17), whilst the duration of their *affliction* was to be four hundred years (Genesis 15:13; Acts 7:6); as it happened we read:

'And it came to pass, at the end of the four hundred and thirty years, *even the self-same day it came to pass,* that all the hosts of the Lord went out from the land of Egypt' (Exodus 12:41).

That this deliverance was the result of agonising prayer may be seen from the Lord's word to Moses, 'I have surely seen the affliction of my people which are in Egypt, and *have heard their cry* by reason of their taskmasters; for I know their sorrows, and I am come down to deliver them out of the hand of the Egyptians' (Exodus 3:7-8).

For the Christian, prayer and praise should not be sporadic, as Paul counselled the Thessalonian believers, 'Be joyful *always*; pray *continually*; give thanks in *all circumstances*' (1 Thessalonians 5:16-18 NIV). These three very brief verses would encourage us to be assiduous in these exercises, and not to 'be weary in well doing', for, 'in due season we shall reap, if we faint not' (Galatians 6:9).

This last possibility was foreseen in the Israelites' conflict with Amalek at the commencement of their wilderness experiences. When they lacked bread, the Lord gave them manna without fail; water was supplied from the smitten Rock continually, but victory over Amalek called for uninterrupted lifting of holy hands on the part of Moses! It was a wearying business and 'Moses hands *were* heavy';

but 'Aaron and Hur stayed up his hands, the one on the one side, and the other on the other side; and his hands were steady until the going down of the sun' (Exodus 17:12). Instead of the fortunes of the battle fluctuating according to Moses' strength, this fellowship of prayer ensured that 'Joshua discomfited Amalek' (v.13). The fleshly element calls for constant vigilance!

'That men ought always to pray and not to faint' was the primary lesson of the Lord's parable of the widow, who sought justice at the bar of the unjust judge, who 'feared not God, nor regarded man' (Luke 18:2). We are to assume that she firmly persisted with her plea, since the judge said, 'Though I fear not God, nor regard man, yet because this widow troubleth me, I will avenge her lest by her continual coming she weary me.' And the Lord said, 'Hear what the unjust judge saith; and shall not God avenge His own elect, which cry day and night unto Him, *though He bear long with them?* I tell you He will avenge them speedily' (Luke 18:1-8).

The examples we have chosen to encourage us to wait upon God are but few among many, and James viewing the long-term prospect, gave some down-to-earth advice as he wrote, 'Be patient brethren unto the coming of the Lord, behold the husbandman waiteth for the precious fruit of the earth, and hath long patience for it until he receive the early and the latter rain. Be ye also patient, stablish your heart, for the Coming of the Lord draweth nigh' (James 5:7-8).

That the purposes of God will be accomplished

according to His sovereign will is confirmed by Isaiah's prophecy, which reminds us that sometimes they are being fulfilled even at the time we lay the matter before Him. He writes, 'before they call, I will answer: and while they are yet speaking, I will hear' (Isaiah 65:24). This does not permit us to be negligent by saying, 'Whatever is to be will be' after the manner of the fatalist. The Lord's blessings are not to be taken for granted, and all revealed truth testifies to the fact that He desires that His people heed the exhortation of the Hebrew Epistle: 'Let us therefore come boldly unto the throne of grace, that we may obtain mercy, and find grace to help in time of need' (Hebrews 4:16). As the Bridegroom of the Song of Songs expresses Himself, 'let me see thy countenance, *let me hear thy voice; for thy voice is sweet*, and thy countenance *is* comely' (Song of Solomon 2:14).

But the common circumstance is to bring the current problem to the Lord and experience His timely help, and as in the example of Leah, it is in times of stress or affliction that the merciful intervention of the Lord for His servant is in answer to his plea.

King David, in spite of his exalted station was not immune from the trials of life. His own son, Absalom, by his persistent treachery, was for long a 'thorn in his side.' As he saw his son's power over the people rivalling his own, he then fled for his life and the experience prompted him to write the 3rd Psalm and record the Lord's goodness to him in his trying ordeal, saying, 'Thou O Lord *art* a shield for me...I cried unto the Lord and *he heard me out of his holy hill* Selah' (v.4).

As if family problems were not enough for the future king, Saul showed little gratitude to David for all the loyalty he had shown to his father-in-law and sovereign, with his valiant triumphs over the king's enemies. As in the case of Leah, the insiduous sin of jealousy was at the root of the king's hostility to David, and his dexterity with his javelin proved to be too much of a ready solution to his fancied problem on more than one occasion! But as David needed to seek refuge from the king, once more he had recourse to prayer and wrote, 'In my distress I called upon the Lord, and cried unto my God: *He heard my voice* out of his temple, and *my cry came before him,* even to his ears' (Psalm 18:6).

The early days of the church proved to be another period when the jealousy of a people — on this occasion Israel — proved to be the cause of much persecution against this new work of God, and is a fulfilment of Rachel's typical hostility to her sister as we have already suggested.

The dogged determination of the believers to proclaim the gospel at all costs was a mighty vindication of God's guidance as thousands were swept into the Kingdom through the preaching of Peter and his fellow apostles.

By and large the Roman power was neutral in matters which they considered outside their responsibility, but they were amenable to the persuasions of the fanatical priesthood of Israel, if it could be shown that their authority was threatened. They therefore made no attempt to shield the believers when the High Priest and his associates had the apostles incarcerated in the state prison after the demonstration of the Spirit's power seen in the testimony of the Apostles in Solomon's porch (Acts 5:12-16).

The deliverance of Peter coincided with the earnest prayers of the church, and though the Lord heeded their prayers with promptitude, their disbelief at Rhoda's announcement of Peter's release by angelic intervention was a sure sign that at least some of the company under-rated the invincible power of God. His mercy often exceeds our deserts!

The kind of affliction Leah suffered is mercifully compensated by the consolation of answered prayer in similar conditions in the life and witness of the church. There is an unbroken chain of experience in the epistle to the Romans as Paul could trace the steps from the 'tribulation' which he gloried in through grace, to the hope and love of God shed abroad in the hearts of the believers (Romans 5:2-6).

The direct link between affliction, prayer and consolation is seen clearly in the first two chapters of 2 Corinthians. The writer states quite positively, 'our hope of you is steadfast, knowing, that as ye are partakers of the sufferings, so shall ye be also of the consolation (2 Corinthians 1:7).

In those early days of the church, there were not only the material gifts that were acknowledged by Paul for the needy ones he contacted in the course of his ministry on more than one occasion, but he could trace their donor's exercise to their spiritual succour too, saying, 'Ye also helping together by prayer for us' (v.11); implying not only the awareness of need, but as the need was met an expression of gratitude for the Lord's provision. Gratitude was a strong feature in the Apostle's character.

In Leah we see one who prayed, and was as ready to testify of the Lord's goodness by His provision and consolation when the awaited time ran its course.

5

Levi — 'Joined'

'He that is joined unto the Lord is one spirit'
(1 Corinthians 6:17).

I

Some years ago Alpheus Wilkes, a wellknown Christian writer, in the first of a series of articles to appear in the 'Morning Star' prophetic magazine, posed the following rhetorical question:

> 'By what processes may a fallen child of Adam become a member of the Body of Christ, and be changed into the image of Christ from glory to glory?
> (Romans 8:29; 2 Corinthians 3:18)
> 'For no change less perfect than this will suffice, if Christ and he are to *become one* and to remain one throughout the eternal ages — Spirit must become like spirit; soul like soul; body like body. Nothing less can possibly be meant by that organic union which exists between a head and a member of the body.'

The writer was of course referring to the mystical union which exists between Christ and his church; those born of the Spirit through faith in Christ.

When Leah gave birth to her third son by Jacob

and named him Levi (Heb. Joined) the tenuous union between Jacob and herself was in her view strengthened, for she said, 'this time will my husband be joined unto me, because I have born him three sons: therefore was his name called Levi' (Genesis 29:34).

As a type of the church Leah's union with Jacob is important, and serves to illustrate the above New Testament statement by Paul (1 Corinthians 6:17).

It is not our purpose to consider the character of Levi, nor the tribe which bore his name, though it had a special relationship with Jehovah in the priesthood; it is sufficient that we concentrate on the reason for the choice of his name, at the time of his birth.

With names which are suggestive of features of the church, the first four sons of Leah make it clear that though Israel came first in time, the church was the fulfilment of the ultimate purpose of God, embracing in itself Jew and Gentile; a hidden truth made known by Paul to whom it had first been revealed.

> 'Unto me, who am less than the least of all saints, is this grace given, that I should preach among the Gentiles the unsearchable riches of Christ; And to make all *men see* what is the fellowship of the *mystery*,*

*In the NT it denotes not the mysterious (as in the English word) but that which being outside of unassisted natural apprehension, can be known only by Divine revelation, and is made known in a manner and at a time appointed by God, and to those only who are illuminated by the Spirit. In the ordinary

4

which from the beginning of the world hath been hid in God, who created all things by Jesus Christ: To the intent that now unto principalities and powers in heavenly *places* might be known by the church the manifold wisdom of God, According to the eternal purpose which he purposed in Jesus Christ our 'Lord' (Ephesians 3:8-11).

It is suggested that though Israel as a nation is for the present set aside, it was clearly God's purpose that it was to have been Jehovah's earthly wife, quite distinct from the church, Christ's heavenly bride, and will one day enjoy Millennial blessings, and in the 'new earth', with others also.

Writing of Israel's future, Isaiah wrote:

'Fear not; for thou shalt not be ashamed: neither be thou confounded; for thou shalt not be put to shame: for thou shalt forget the shame of thy youth, and shalt not remember the reproach of thy widow-hood any more. For thy Maker *is* thine husband; the 'Lord of hosts'* *is* his name; and thy Redeemer the Holy One of Israel: For a small moment have I forsaken thee: but with great mercies will I gather thee' (Isaiah 54:4, 5, 7).

Jeremiah too saw that in spite of the fact that Israel had lost, for the time being, her destined role, pleaded:

sense a mystery implies knowledge withheld; its spiritual significance is truth revealed' (W E Vine).

*Jehovah Adonai.

'Thou hast played the harlot with many
lovers; yet return again to me, saith the
Lord (*Jehovah*)' (Jeremiah 3:1).

These and many other scriptures give no support
for the views favoured by many of the members of
World Council of Churches that the promises to
Israel are all fulfilled in the church, with no
possibility of Israel enjoying Millennial blessings
independently, as God's earthly people. The danger
inherent in this idea is that God's immutability
apart from His other attributes is called in question,
since it is possible, they affirm, for the Almighty to
change His mind. That God may seem to defer His
plans we can accept, knowing that even this would
be in His mind before His purposes were revealed.
An apparent postponement is something quite
different from an abrogation.

Whatever part Israel and Levi played in the past,
and will do in the future, the significance of Levi's
name has more to do with Christ's relationship to
the Church, and with its eternal bond with Him,
than all else. In the priesthood Levi enjoyed *nearness*
to God, but the Church is *joined* by an eternal bond
to its heavenly Bridegroom.

This union which exists between Christ and His
Church is without question one of its most
important features. It implies that the Church is a
living organism rather than an organisation. That
there has to be organisation at various levels goes
without saying, but by itself this could never have
sustained it, let alone brought it into being.

Its greatest value to mankind is seen in its ability
to welcome into its flock all who are prepared to

acknowledge the Lordship of Christ, Jew or Gentile; this third body, thus formed, no longer recognises old racial barriers, and its members can now live in harmony among themselves through the Divine wisdom.

Paul, the apostle, described the way in which it was brought about in the following passage:

> 'remember that you were ... Gentiles by birth, and called "uncircumcision" by those who call themselves "the circumcision" (that done in the body by the hands of man)—remember that at that time you were separate from Christ, excluded from citizenship in Israel and foreigners to the covenants of the promise, without God and without hope in the world. But now in Christ Jesus you who once were far away have been brought near through the blood of Christ. For he himself is our peace, who has made the two one and has destroyed the barrier, the dividing wall of hostility, by abolishing in his flesh the law with its commandments and regulations. His purpose was to create in himself one new man out of the two, thus making peace' (Ephesians 2:11-15 NIV).

This union between Christ and the church is a matter of supreme mutual importance, and is typically expressed by Leah as she makes her plaintive remark, when she craves a deeper experience of Jacob's affections at the time of Levi's birth. This bond is also illustrated in the Apostle

Paul's treatise on the church in the Ephesian epistle. In this he uses three distinct figures, all of which imply oneness within itself. The strength of the bond pertaining to Christ and the church is, in the nature of the case, intended to be more secure than any figure which portrays it, but nevertheless affords thought provoking lessons.

II

The first simile of the church we will consider is that of a *Building*, described in the Ephesian epistle as follows:

'ye are no more strangers and foreigners, but fellow citizens with the saints, and of the household of God; And are built upon the foundation of the apostles and prophets, Jesus Christ himself being the chief corner *stone*. In whom all the building fitly framed together, groweth into an holy temple of the Lord. In whom ye also are builded together for an habitation of God through the Spirit (Ephesians 2:19-22).

The stated purpose of this mystical building is that it is 'an holy temple of the Lord', and 'an habitation of God through the Spirit'. Such a concept elevates the church to a plane far above any human idea of what it is, or can be; and serves to remind His people that since He is a holy God, and by the atonement of Christ has made the way for them to become morally like Himself, the injunction of Peter becomes imperative, 'as he which hath called you is holy, so be ye holy in all manner of conversation; because it is written, Be ye holy; for I am holy' (1 Peter 1:15-16). In New Testament days the 'household' consisted of the family and servants of the master; and it is within the confines of the church we 'serve the Lord Christ' and 'by love serve one another' (Colossians 3:24; Galatians 5:13). This 'household' is drawn from both Jew and Gentile, which causes Paul to state that the Gentiles to whom he addressed himself in the main, were 'no more strangers, but fellow citizens with the saints'.

All this confirms that the Christian is, perforce, joined to Christ, the foundation; otherwise he cannot make the claim to be one, but equally Jew and Gentile are 'joined in one body by the Cross'. The seemingly impossible is achieved in His own inimical way.

A building suggests a preconceived plan; in the case of the church it was designed 'According to the eternal purpose which He purposed in Christ Jesus our Lord' (Eph. 3:11). If it could be said of Abraham that he looked for a city 'with foundations whose architect and builder is God' (Heb. 11:10 NIV), how much more can such Divine planning be assumed and confirmed for the Church?

In the Ephesian passage the building was said to be 'built upon the foundation of Apostles and prophets', an allusion to its human 'founder members' (if one may use such a term for the sake of convenience). Paul, however, elsewhere makes an important reservation as to the relative importance of this claim, in saying 'I have laid the foundation, and another buildeth thereon. But let every man take heed how he buildeth thereupon.

For *other foundation* can no man lay than that is laid, which is *Jesus Christ'* (1 Corinthians 3:10-11).

The final statement in no way invalidates the God-given part Paul played in the visible expression of the church. It was he who revealed its 'hidden mystery'; whose evangelical labours contributed vastly to its growth, and whose inspired writings remain for its guidance, not least in the ordering of the local church.

The first notion given to man of the part Christ was to assume as the church's rock foundation was when with the disciples at Caesarea Philippi He put the question to them, 'Whom do men say that I the Son of Man, am?' And then more directly, after the disciples had given the answers reflecting current opinion, 'But whom say ye that I am?' to which Simon Peter replied, 'Thou art the Christ, the Son of the Living God', and to which the Lord responded, 'Blessed art thou, Simon Bar-jona: for flesh and blood hath not revealed *it* unto thee, but my Father which is in heaven, And I say unto thee, That thou art Peter (a little stone), and upon this rock (Himself) I will build my church; and the gates of hell shall not prevail against it' (Matthew 16:13-18). Peter's confession of the Divinity of His person, evoked the Lord's revelation about His purpose.

The impression this incident made upon Peter must have been considerable, so much so that he furnishes us with many valuable lessons as he writes of the spiritual house of the church in his first Epistle (1 Peter 2:4-10).

(1) We come by faith to Christ the living stone—

(2) Believers are themselves lively (living) stones incorporated.

(3) Christ is the Chief Corner Stone for our faith. He was 'disallowed indeed of men (Israel), but chosen of God *and* precious' (v.4). 'The same is made head of the corner' (v.7).

(4) This 'house' is 'an holy priesthood to offer up spiritual sacrifices' (v.5), a 'royal priesthood', an 'holy nation' to 'show forth praises of Him who hath called you out of darkness into his marvellous light' (v.9). In this Peter is seen to enlarge on Paul's brief description of the 'spiritual house' as he introduces the priesthood of the believer who glorifies God by his spiritual sacrifices (i.e. of praise and worship in the local church).

As individuals we heed Christ's words and are said to build our house on the Rock (Matthew 7:24-25). In the aggregate we gather in His name as a church built upon the Rock, for His glory.

Among the various references from Scripture to the church's foundation Paul's symbol of the Rock (1 Corinthians 10:1-6) though intended as a cautionary 'example' (i.e. 'pattern in the ethical sense'—Vine), nevertheless gives a striking illustration of Christ's claim to be nothing less than that.

The quotation Paul refers to concerns Israel at Horeb soon after the Exodus. The people murmured against Moses for lack of water and he was instructed to 'smite the rock and there shall come water out of it' (Exodus 17:6). This evidently prefigured Christ's sufferings at Calvary, 'yet we did esteem him, stricken, *smitten of God* and afflicted' (Isaiah 53:4) and apart from its literal benefit to the people at Horeb, this gushing stream is a symbol of the Holy Spirit in the church (John 7:39) issuing from 'that spiritual Rock that followed them, and that Rock was Christ.' (1 Corinthians 10:4)

Later at Kadesh Barnea towards the end of Israel's wilderness wanderings, the people once more needed water, and again, 'chode with Moses' for bringing them out of Egypt, forgetting meanwhile God's earlier provision for them (Numbers 20); on this occasion He told Moses to 'speak to the Rock', that the water might once more be forthcoming. Alas, in anger, Moses struck the rock a second time and, though the water issued from it, his hasty act of disobedience caused him to forfeit the right to enter Canaan.

An interesting distinction is made in the Hebrew between the first and second mention of the Rock. In the first passage it is a rock without further description, but in the second it is an elevated rock (Youngs). Paul's Messianic reference to it in 1 Corinthians 10 authorises us to relate the stricken Rock of Exodus 17 to the atoning work of Christ upon the cross, and the elevated Rock of Numbers 20 to the resurrection, and ascension of Christ with the related truth of the coming of the Spirit at Pentecost (John 16:7).

It need not surprise us that Christ is also the 'Chief Corner Stone' of this spiritual edifice. 'He *is* all and in all' (Colossians 3:11) with His many offices, names and titles, and soon to be 'King of Kings and Lord of Lords', in the day of His power

(Revelation 19:12-16).

The Oxford English Dictionary definition of a corner-stone is, 'one of those forming quoin or a salient angle of a wall' (fig.) 'indispensable thing or part'. This unification of parts can only be achieved by the 'unity of the Spirit', and can relate only to those who are first in union with Christ, or to quote our earlier text 'He that is joined unto the Lord is one Spirit' (1 Corinthians 6:17). We cannot emphasise too strongly that the 'new birth' by faith in Christ is the only basis of unity, in spite of the efforts of the many historic churches to effect a unity on a specious liberal basis, commonly known as 'Church unity', a question more fully dealt with in a later chapter and in Appendix 'C', q.v.

III

The most familiar of all emblems of the church is that of the Bride (Ephesians 5:23-33). It is the subject of prophecy and typology from its inception in Eden to the Marriage Supper of the Lamb (Revelation 19); and just as the building must be contiguous with its foundation, and a body is joined to its head, so there cannot be a bride without a bridegroom. Union is the essential feature.

In this Ephesians passage it would be difficult to decide whether the marriage union is illustrative of the church, or whether the reverse is intended. Both are treated as subjects of supreme importance, and complement each other; in the Ephesian context we favour the first.

The first point to claim our attention is that of the

church's subjection to Christ, its Head (v.23). In acknowledging the husband as head of the family, the wife demonstrates in a practical manner this truth, 'even as Christ is head of the church' (v.23). This dictum is given in the interests of an orderly household, and even more important as to the ordering of the affairs of the church. Whether the Christian is dealing with the elders of his local church or in the relationship of the individual to the State, nowhere is delegated authority to be flouted except, of course, when that authority conflicts with the revealed will of God for His people (Mark 12:17; Romans 13:1; 1 Corinthians 14:33; Colossians 3:22, etc.). Even when the Apostle directs a word to husbands it is to remind their wives that they are the recipients of his love 'even as Christ loved the church and gave Himself for it.' The measure of His love is to be valued by the vastness of His sacrifice. Peter describes the character of the union with sensitivity, using the phrase 'heirs together of the grace of life' (1 Peter 3:7). The degree in which the wife is to be 'nourished and cherished' is likewise governed by the Divine standard, 'even as the Lord the church' (Ephesians 5:29).

The word 'cherish' expresses the idea of 'fostering with tender care' (Vine), and for an apostolic example, Paul claimed that both he and his associates when they evangelised among the Thessalonians, 'were gentle among you, even as a nurse (lit. nursing mother) cherisheth her children' (1 Thessalonians 2:7).

From the moment of the church's inception at Pentecost, its true objective has been to eagerly anticipate the Lord's return. This hope of the church is clearly stated to be the motivation for the believer's endeavour to live a sanctified life (1 John 3:3).

> 'That he might present it to himself a glorious church, not having spot, or wrinkle, or any such thing; but that it might be holy and without blemish' (Ephesians 5:26-27).

Or as Paul writes elsewhere:

> 'blameless and harmless, the sons of God, without rebuke, in the midst of a crooked and perverse nation, among whom ye shine as lights in the world' (Philippians 2:15).

This spiritual cleansing 'by The Word' is not intended to foster the abnormal but rather the normal Christian life, in spite of its demanding high standards. Our Lord taught this by His own example before the Cross; that all needed to submit to the figurative washing of feet, or as our Ephesian passage says, 'the washing of water by the Word' as the antidote for our walk through a defiling world (John 13:4-17). Following His example we serve one another!

Closely associated with the idea of a sanctified walk on the part of members of the church is that of living independent of the baneful influences of the world order (Cosmos) i.e.

> 'The present conditions of human affairs, in alienation and opposition to God' (Vine).

This is not to advocate the monastic life; the spirit

of the world cannot be excluded by living in a confined community. Rather it is conducting the essential affairs of life according to the spirit and principles laid down by the Master, and following His example.

The foremost idea governing both the Christian marriage union and that between Christ and the church is of fellowship.

In creation God said, 'It is not good that the man should be alone: I will make an help meet for him' (Genesis 2:18). The following verses describing Adam's activities in the classification and naming of the animal creation, include the following significant phrase, 'for Adam there was not found an help meet for him.' Clearly it was not within the order of the animal creation that a suitable companion was to be found for the man. Rather it called for a special, creative act on the part of God. It is seen to be a combination of the human and Divine as God caused a 'deep sleep' to fall upon Adam (v.21), that the answer to man's need was to be found. In like manner the incarnation of Christ, which made possible His atoning sacrifice at Calvary, was the basis for the higher union between Christ and His bride, the church. Well might Paul remark 'This is a great mystery: but I speak concerning Christ and the church' (Ephesians 5:32). Far from being a product of mankind in his supposed development and search for truth, Paul sees the Christian as part of a new beginning. 'if any man be in Christ, he is a new creature (creation): old things have passed away; behold, all things are become new' (2 Corinthians 5:17). Creation has to give place to redemption as the Divine priority.

IV

The third concept of the church from the Ephesian epistle is that of *'a body'*, over which Christ is the Head. Of the three this is the most widely treated by a range of texts from this Epistle, and an even larger passage from 1 Corinthians ch.12, to which we will refer.

We are first told that God 'gave him (Christ) to *be head of all* things to the church, Which is *his body*, the fulness (complement) of him that filleth all in all' (Ephesians 1:22-23). These verses are preceded by Paul's prayer that the church might grasp to some extent the greatness and *glory of its Head*.

This final clause on the 'fulness' of Christ places Him in terms of *equality with the Father*, 'who is above all, and through all, and in you all' (Ephesians 4:6), a truth which many of the modern cults blindly deny.

The burden of Paul's prayer is that our first concern should be to experience a 'knowledge of the Father of glory' (Ephesians 1:17) since *knowing Him* by faith is the secret of eternal life (John 17:3). This carries with it a two-fold bond of security for as he says elsewhere, 'rather we *are known of God'* (Galatians 4:9).

He then prays that we may have understanding of 'the hope to which he has called us' NIV (v.18), explained elsewhere as being 'with Christ and like Him eternally' (1 John 3:2).

This awareness embraces not only what the church has in Christ, but also *what Christ possesses in the church*, 'the riches of the glory of his inheritance in the saints' (Ephesians 1:18).

Further he prays that we may know the 'exceeding greatness of his power to usward who believe,' a power 'wrought (exerted) in Christ when he raised him from the dead, and set him at his own right hand in the heavenlies' (Ephesians 1:19-20).

It is only after this that the Apostle reveals *the vast powers vested in the Head of the body.* To be united to such an One is honour indeed!

We are then told of *Christ's power and authority,* but let it be noted that we are never allowed to scale its limitless heights, but merely to be informed of lesser powers over which He excels, which are great in themselves!

We must accept the fact that our English translation gives but slight indication of Christ's resources, in saying He is 'far above *all principality, and power, and might, and dominion,* and everything that is named, not only in this world, but also in that which is to come' (Ephesians 1:21). In the light of such a revelation we are reminded of Joseph Addison's hymn:

> 'Transported with the view I'm lost
> In wonder, love and praise.'

Various Bible 'helps' enable us to understand what Paul meant when he wrote these words. They suggest according to Greek usage, that the *'principalities'* are 'angels, that excel in strength' (Psalm 103:20), both good and evil. The next word *'power'* has reference to delegated power, such as a Minister of the Crown has in government. Again it is not limited to human agencies. *'Might'* (the same as in Ephesians 3:16) is that available to us through the Spirit in our *'inner man'* which describes the mind of man in general. Lastly, *'dominion'* refers to 'a lower order of angelic powers' (Vine) but nonetheless considerable in themselves.

As we consider this inspired prayer of the Apostle, we are conscious of the *unlimited power and wisdom* invested in Christ *as Head of the church*, which human language fails utterly to express; nevertheless the Lord sees the body as an essential part of the plan of man's redemption; there could in fact be no redemption without it. This is possibly reflected in Paul's words, 'the eye cannot say unto the hand, I have no need of thee: nor the *head to the feet*, I have no need of you' (1 Corinthians 12:21). Such a saying is based on the compulsion of love without regard to the Lord's self-sufficiency.

The next reference in Ephesians to 'the body' takes into account its broad based membership, consisting of Jew and Gentile. As the Apostle of the Gentiles, Paul had a vested interest in this aspect of the body of Christ, and reminded his Corinthian converts, 'Ye know that ye were Gentiles, carried away unto these dumb idols', and writing as a Jewish convert he says, 'For by one Spirit are we all baptized into one body, whether we be Jews or Gentiles' (1 Corinthians 12:2; 13). In all ages the native born Jew, as distinct from his Christian counterpart, has been strictly insular, never classifying himself with other than the descendants of Jacob. As Paul reminded his Ephesian converts, they were once 'aliens from the commonwealth of Israel, and strangers from the covenants of promise, having no hope, and without God in the world' (Ephesians 2:12). During the pre-Christian history of Israel any affinity with the neighbouring pagan nations called for God's judgment upon them, and since that time, the one and only union between Jew and Gentile is within the fold of the church of God, and within which the Gentiles once 'far off' are now 'made nigh'; once enemies but now 'at peace' with the racial barrier broken down in Christ. The seemingly impossible obstacle, 'the law' being removed finds 'both reconciled unto God in one body by the Cross, (God) having slain the enmity thereby' (Ephesians 2:13-16).

Such a Gentile inclusion in the church, though hidden in the writings of the prophets, at times found the Jewish converts reverting to their former practices within the sphere of the church, as the corrective teachings contained in the Epistles of Galatians and the Hebrews reveal.

It needed a Paul with a special dispensation from God to unfold the hidden mystery of the Church, in order that all should 'understand my knowledge', he wrote, 'in the mystery of Christ.' Claiming no credit to himself he continued, 'it is now revealed unto his holy apostles and prophets by the Spirit; that the Gentiles should be fellow-heirs and of the same body, and partakers of His promise in Christ by the gospel' (Ephesians 3:1-6).

Paul terms this 'a unity of the Spirit' (Ephesians 4:3) which must be kept in the bond of peace, since 'there is one body, and one Spirit, even as ye are called in one of your calling; One Lord, one faith, one baptism, hopeOne God and Father of all' (vs.4-6).

The unity here mentioned is of God the Spirit's ordering, and can apply only to believers who have been 'created in Christ Jesus', and 'made nigh by the blood of Christ' (Ephesians 2:10; 13), as were the Ephesian believers.

For further confirmation of this truth, we refer once more to the first Corinthian epistle (ch.12) which says, 'For as the body is one, and hath many members, and all the members of that one body being many, are one body, so also is Christ' (v.12) '...and all given the one Spirit to drink' (v.13 NIV). The body's diversity in unity is stated and is inverted in two verses in this context, which read:

'The body is not one member, but many' (v.14).

'Now are they many members, but one body' (v.20).

The next group of texts (Ephesians 4:11:15) tells us that the 'one body' is organic as to its nature rather than an organisation, and as such is continually growing and developing, not necessarily in numbers, but as a living spiritual body; though its membership is, in fact, increasing at the same time.

The edification of the body, as it is termed, is assisted by Spirit-gifted individuals who at the first were apostles and prophets who spoke from God before the New Testament canon became the church's guide and charter. After this the gifts were 'evangelists' (messengers of the Gospel), 'pastors' (for the caring of the flock of God) and 'teachers' (to inculcate the truths of the Word) that sound doctrine might be the means for 'the edifying of the body of Christ' (Ephesians 4:12).

This process is described in symbolic language by Paul, 'speaking the truth in love, we will in all things grow up into him, who is the Head, that is Christ. From him, the whole body, joined and held together by every supporting ligament, grows and builds itself up in love, as each part does its work' (Ephesians 4:15-16 NIV).

It is not out of place to refer once more to the Corinthian epistle with its warning which had special application to that church, 'That there should be no schism in the body; but that the members should have the same care one for another. And whether one member suffer, all the members suffer with it; Now ye are the body of Christ, and members in particular' (1 Corinthians 12:25-27).

Where there is schism there is at some point a breakdown of truth. In Corinth it was defined in 1 Corinthians 1:10-12, and if we deplore the divisions of today it is equally because the truth of the Word has been abandoned. The remedy is clearly to recover the truth and thereby restore the unity. Merely coming together without a true doctrinal basis can only spell confusion, and in spite of the specious claims that such action is evidence of 'a movement of the Spirit', its protagonists are dealing with effects rather than the causes of division.

To summarise, the meaningful union with Jacob which Leah desired at the birth of Levi, this suggests to us the living bond between Christ and the church; the fellowship of Jew and Gentile within its fold, and 'the unity of the Spirit in the bond of peace' as a means of achieving the only possible degree of unity which will stand the test of time in the church of God.

6

Judah — 'Praise'

'By Him therefore, let us offer the sacrifice of praise to God continually' (Hebrews 13:15; John 4:24).

'And she (Leah) conceived again, and bare a son: and she said, Now will I praise the Lord: therefore she called his name Judah, and left bearing'
(Genesis 29:35).

The prophetic words by Leah at the birth of Judah is one of the wonders of Divine inspiration, when we consider the fulfilment of it in the short, medium and long time spans, the last being yet future.

Judah has more to do with praise than any other tribe. The greatest descendant of Judah, apart from the Saviour, with whom we associate the subject of praise, is King David 'the sweet Psalmist of Israel' (2 Samuel 23:1).

He not only wrote about one half of the Hebrew Psalter, which among the rest were used in the temple worship, where, 'four thousand praised the Lord with the instruments I made, *said David*, to praise *therewith*' (1 Chronicles 23:5), but in a masterly manner he organised the courses of the singers as fully detailed in the chapters 23 to 25 of the same book.

His reputation as a singer brought him to the

court of King Saul, where his talent may appear to have been wasted, not because of any failure on David's part, but rather because of the fearful jealousy of the insecure king.

Apart from his later public involvement in the task of bringing praise to God within the conditions prevailing in the Temple worship, many of his odes reflected his response to God's over-ruling in his personal life.

The lengthy Psalm 18, as its headnote tells us, was one of thanksgiving for God's deliverances, especially from the hand of Saul.

The well loved Psalm 103, praises God for His restoring grace after times of failure (vs.3-5).

Psalm 108 is an account of David's confidence in God and prophetically anticipates conditions during the millennial reign of Christ when Judah, represented in Him, will be the Lawgiver (v.8).

The Hallel Psalms (113 to 118) as their name suggests, were *Songs of Praise* and together with Psalm 136 were regularly used during the Jewish festival periods, and it is to be expected that when Jesus and His disciples 'sang an hymn' between the Passover Supper and the agony of Gethsemane, it would have been from this group of Psalms.

We note the striking similarity between Psalm 113:5-9 and the latter part of Hannah's song of praise at the birth of Samuel (1 Samuel 2:8); whilst Psalm 114 reminds us of the honour conferred on the tribe of Judah by locating the Temple in its territory, and so, 'Judah is His sanctuary' (v.2) where the praises of God were a marked feature.

The subject matter of these 'praise Psalms'

ranges from Israel's deliverance from the Egyptian bondage (114:1) to the restoration of Israel at a time yet future, when the nation will, at last, cry in unison, Thou art my God, and I will praise Thee. 'O give thanks unto the Lord for He is good, for His mercy endureth for ever' (Psalm 118:28-29); so ends the Hallel.

It is from this last Psalm that we read the significant phrase, 'Blessed be He that cometh in the name of the Lord' (v.26), which affords us one of the key verses of Scripture, for the right understanding of God's prophetic plan for Israel. It was first used by the children and the multitude in the territory of Judah when the Saviour rode upon the ass into Jerusalem on that memorable day, commonly known as Palm Sunday, just five days before the crucifixion (Matthew 21:15). The disciples had been told by the Lord to fetch the animal, which was to be identified by certain precise features (Matthew 21:2) and as He entered Jerusalem the thronging crowd, present for the Passover, pressed along 'before and behind' crying 'Blessed *is* he that cometh in the name of the Lord' (Matthew 21:9).

In this manner was fulfilled Zechariah's ancient prophecy:

> 'Tell the daughter of Sion, Behold thy
> King cometh unto thee meek and sitting
> upon an ass, and a colt, the foal of an ass'
> (Matthew 21:5; Zechariah 9:9).

But although this prediction had been carried out to the letter, this adulation of the people was but a partial fulfilment of Psalm 118:26. The gospel narrative makes a distinction between the praising people who had followed the Lord, and the obdurate ruling class, with the Jewish religious order, which desired nothing more than to be spared such seemingly vulgar excitement!

We read 'the city was moved crying, Who is this?, (Matthew 21:10) whilst the multitude said, This is Jesus the Prophet of Nazareth of Galilee (v.11). On the one hand was the devoted remnant of Israel, ready to acknowledge its Messiah, before the time, and, on the other, the casuistic priesthood, and the corrupt occupying power who would connive, and agree to crucify Israel's rightful King.

If, as we suggest, we are to regard this Palm Sunday demonstration as nothing more than a partial fulfilment of Psalm 118, we are obliged to indicate when the prophecy will be fully realised. Our Lord indicated such a time when He quoted it after Israel's final rejection of Himself prior to the crucifixion as His final warning to the apostate nation:

> 'Ye shall not see me henceforth, till ye
> shall say, Blessed is he that cometh in the
> name of the Lord' (Matthew 23:39).

This severance of Israel from Divine favour for the time being was from that moment complete. In a matter of weeks what must be seen as the most significant change in human affairs was begun. The Crucifixion, the Resurrection and the Ascension of the risen Christ, with the coming of the Holy Spirit to indwell members of the church which He had founded in fulfilment of His promise to Peter, followed, in that order, rapidly. Very soon the Gentiles were brought into blessing on equal terms with the earlier Jewish converts who comprised the church's founder members. Incidentally there can be no reconciliation with God on the part of Israel until the church is removed from the scene at the time of the rapture at the coming of the Lord. Israel will then be seen to be in the centre of world events. At first the nation will acknowledge the antichrist, as part of a trinity of evil, and as a result will suffer untold sorrows later when it will be, in the words of the prophet, 'a day of darkness and of gloominess, a day of clouds and of thick darkness' (Joel 2:2). Eventually, as a repentant mourning nation it will be reconciled to the One it crucified when He appears in glory in a form which they cannot fail to recognise, (Zechariah 12:9-10), and as Isaiah promised the nation, 'He shall appear to your joy' (ch.66:5). At that time Psalm 118 will be upon the lips of the remnant of Israel in the following words:

'The Lord hath chastened me sore: but he hath not given me over unto death. Open to me the gates of righteousness: I will go into them, *and I will praise the Lord*' (vs.18-19): '*I will praise thee*; for thou hast heard me, and art become my salvation.'

'The stone *which* the builders refused is become the head stone of the corner. This is the Lord's doing; and it is marvellous in our eyes. This is the day *which* the Lord hath made, we will rejoice and be glad in it' (vs.21-24).

'Blessed is he that cometh in the name of the Lord' (v.26).

'Thou art my God, and *I will praise thee*.

Thou art my God, I will exalt Thee' (v.28).

With these praises on their lips will Israel's remnant welcome their Redeemer King, after centuries of persecution, judgments, and dispersion among the nations. At last the promises made to Abraham and his descendants will have been honoured.

The last reference in Scripture to Judah, is associated with the greatest and most exuberant paean which will ever be heard in all time, and could occur only in the heavenly regions.

On that occasion the Eternal God will be seen to occupy the throne of Heaven where He will wield undisputed power and authority. In His right hand is a seven-sealed book, which in the circumstances of its appearing at the time of coming judgments, would seem to confirm Walter Scott's view that it is the record of *'The Revelation of God's Purposes and Counsel concerning the World'*, as He is about to authorise the opening of the successive seals.

The seer observes in a state of distress, 'I wept much, because no one had been found worthy to open the book, nor to regard it. And one of the elders said to me, Do not weep, Behold *the Lion which is of the tribe of Judah*, the root of David, has overcome (so as) to open the book and its seven seals' (Revelation 5:4-5 Darby).

As the writer continues the symbolic language changes, and instead of Christ appearing as 'The Lion of the tribe of Judah', he says:

> 'I beheld, and, lo, in the midst of the throne and of the four beasts, and in the midst of the elders, stood a Lamb (lit. a

young lamb) as it had been slain, having
seven horns and seven eyes, which are
the seven Spirits of God sent forth into all
the earth. And He came and took the book
out of the right hand of him that sat upon
the throne' (vs.6-7).

'*And they sung a new song* saying, Thou art
worthy to take the book, and to open the
seals thereof: for thou wast slain, and
hast redeemed us to God by thy blood out
of every kindred, and tongue, and people
and nation; and hast made us unto our
God kings and priests: and we shall reign
on the earth' (vs.9-10).

Here there is a vast concourse,

'the number of them was ten thousand
times ten thousand, and thousands of
thousands; Saying with a loud voice,
Worthy is the Lamb that was slain to
receive power, and riches, and wisdom,
and strength, and honour, and glory, and
blessing' (vs.11-12).

Finally the entire creation adds its tribute to
Eternal God and His Son, our Redeemer, consisting
of 'every creature in heaven and on the earth, and
under the earth, and such as are in the sea, and all
that are in them, heard I saying,

'Blessing, and honour, and glory, and
power, *be* unto him that sitteth upon the
throne, and unto the Lamb for ever and
ever. And the four beasts said, Amen,
And the four and twenty elders fell down
and worshipped him that liveth for ever

and ever' (vs.13-14).
The Lion of Judah is therefore none other than the
Lamb of Calvary, Lord of creation, God of
judgment, and Redeemer of all that come to Him in
the obedience of faith.

II

At all times in the Christian church, the subject of
praise has received a place of prominence as part of
its worship, and rightly so.

Whether or not the modern trend towards the
proliferation of hymn books in their various forms
is good, is an open question; many merely duplicate
what has already been available under other titles.
And what is a cause for concern in the contemporary
scene is the neglect of soundly based hymns by time
honoured writers and composers only to be
replaced by much that is trivial to say the least, and
dealing with a limited range of subjects worthy of
our praise; and which in fact dishonours the Lord by
its neglect of His rich endowments, which were the
subject matter of past ages.

Often the distinction between spiritual praise
and 'singing' is ignored; the Lord's intention for His
people is the expression of enlightened spiritual
truth in the hymns which are used. Music and
singing for the sake of its artistic merits does little
for the spiritual development of the Christian life.
In all things God must be glorified, and the church
edified by the sublimity of the themes employed.
His transcendent Person and his inscrutable ways
should be the test of excellence in this matter.

When the early church became first aware of the spiritual revolution which had involved it through the redemptive work of Christ, and its own unique calling, utterly distinct from anything Israel has experienced for about 1500 years, together with the fact of the Holy Spirit's presence as 'a Guide, a Comforter, bequeathed, with us to dwell', it causes no surprise to read that in fellowship they 'did eat their meat with gladness and singleness of heart. Praising God, and having favour with all the people' (Acts 2:46-47). The shadows and types of Judaism had passed, to be replaced with that which was first and foremost in the mind and purposes of God.

At the time of the Saviour's first coming, among the faithful remnant of Israel there were those who had a God-given prescience of what the Lord was about to do. As Elizabeth, John the Baptist's mother, came to Mary the mother of the Lord, before the forerunner's birth, she testified, 'as soon as the voice of thy salutation sounded in mine ears, the babe leaped in my womb for joy' (Luke 1:44), and as for Mary herself, she began her song of praise, 'My soul doth magnify the Lord, and my spirit hath rejoiced in God my Saviour' (Luke 1:46-47). Even the angelic host were 'praising God, and saying, Glory to God in the highest, and on earth peace, goodwill toward men' (Luke 2:13-14). The incarnation was the first great step in the plan of redemption.

In the gospel story the Saviour could speak to the Samaritan woman of 'true worshippers' in contrast to anything she could have known before, and continued 'God is a Spirit: and they that worship him must worship *him* in Spirit and in truth' (John 4:23-24). One marvels that another who had so recently felt the healing power of Christ as his sight was given him could say, 'if any man be a *worshipper* of God, and doeth His will, him He heareth' (John 9:31). These instances were but an earnest of what was soon to follow. Paul could describe the transition from law to grace as follows, 'we are the circumcision, which *worship God* in the spirit, and *rejoice* in Christ Jesus, and have no confidence in the flesh' (Philippians 3:3).

Nor is this rejoicing confined to the welcome seasons of public worship. James seems to encourage us to praise the Lord in the hurly burly of life, 'Is any among you afflicted? let him pray. Is any merry? let him sing psalms' (James 5:13). Paul too could advise 'the giving of thanks' in preference to the 'foolish talking' of the worldly mind. (Ephesians 5:4).

In our Saviour's darkest hours before the Cross, as He celebrated with His disciples, the feast based on His passion, 'when they had sung an hymn, they went out to the Mount of Olives' (Matthew 26:30). Furthermore, as can be gathered from the Psalm of the Cross, He could say as the triumph was about to be evidenced, 'in the midst of the congregation will I praise thee'...'My praise *shall be* of thee in the great congregation.'...'The meek shall eat and be satisfied; they shall praise the Lord that seek him' (Hebrews 2:12; Psalm 22:22; 25-26). We may have some faint reflection of this Divine joy in the story of the first church in Europe at its beginning, with Paul and Silas in prison at Philippi. With beaten backs in strict confinement, 'at midnight Paul and Silas prayed, and sang praises unto God.' What a witness as 'the prisoners heard them' (Acts 16:25). The tortures of life have proved to be no barrier to the effective praise of God on the part of the Christian, as all history confirms.

We owe it to the Divine wisdom that whilst, as we have insisted, the Church is entirely distinct from the Hebrew connection, nevertheless it is able to borrow the words of praise to God from the ancient writings and recognise their spiritual content, and the ready application of them to the Christian's need in worship. What is even more striking is the prophetic word anticipating such a situation. For instance, Paul writing to the Romans, basically a Gentile church but with a few Jewish members (e.g. Romans 16:11) says, 'Jesus Christ was a minister of the circumcision for the truth of God, to confirm the promises *made* unto the fathers: and that the Gentiles might glorify God for *his* mercy: as it is written, For this cause I will confess to thee among the Gentiles, and sing unto thy name. And again he saith, Rejoice, ye Gentiles with his people. And again, Praise the Lord, all ye Gentiles; and laud him, all ye people' (Romans 15:8-11). This doubtless adds weight to the Apostle Paul's injunction, 'Speaking to yourselves in psalms and hymns and spiritual songs, singing and making melody in your heart to the Lord' (Ephesians 3:19; Colossians 3:17). Needless to say, praise is not entirely singing, the verbal expression in the Spirit's power is entirely edifying to the hearer. We may remind ourselves in this connection that among the Levitical offerings the peace offering (lit. Sacrifice), which emphasised the human response to the restored relationship between the worshipper and God, is the only one which reflected this idea of thanksgiving for obvious reasons. So we read, 'If he offer it for a thanksgiving, then he shall offer with the sacrifice of *thanksgiving unleavened* cakes. Besides the cakes, he shall offer *for* his offering *leavened* bread with the sacrifice of *thanksgiving* of his peace offerings and the flesh of the sacrifice of his peace offering for *thanksgiving* shall be eaten the same day that it is offered' (Leviticus 7:12; 13; 15). That it is offered with leavened bread suggests the imperfections of our praises and thanksgiving whilst still in the body. We may make so much of our blessings and forget the claims of the Blesser in our adoration.

Paul doubtless had this offering in mind when he wrote words which would have a familiar ring in the ears of his Hebrew friends, 'By him therefore let us offer the *sacrifice of praise* to God continually, that is, the fruit of *our* lips giving thanks to his name' (Hebrews 13:15).

Peter, too, writing to the scattered Hebrew believers wrote, 'But ye *are* a chosen generation, a royal priesthood, an holy nation, a peculiar people; that ye should show forth the praises of him who hath called you out of darkness into his marvellous light' (1 Peter 2:9). He aptly summed it up with his injunction, 'If any man speak, *let him speak* as the oracles of God; if any man minister, *let him do it* as of the ability which God giveth: that God in all things may be glorified through Jesus Christ, to whom be praise and dominion for ever and ever, Amen' (1 Peter 4:11).

An event of some significance is that after the birth of her fourth son 'Leah called his name Judah; *and left bearing*' (Genesis 29:35).

Some years were to elapse before Leah gave birth to other sons; the hiatus periods of Scripture, such as this, are very significant as we shall see as the story develops.

7

Dan — God hath Judged

'There shall be great distress in the land'
(Luke 21:23).

During Leah's fertile years, like the early church, she had passed from 'affliction' to 'praise', signified by the names she had given her sons. Now she was to share the grief of Rachel, whom she had unwittingly deposed through the action of Laban, by, herself, becoming barren.

Scripture does not indicate whether or not this turn of events prompted Rachel to set in motion a scheme by which she could attempt to recover the affections of Jacob once more.

Her idea of surrogation which was to be effected by offering her handmaid Bilhah to Jacob meant that, if successful, she would be able to claim such sons as were born to the handmaid as her own.

This plan probably suggested itself to her, following the example of Jacob's grandmother, Sarai, who connived with Abram to take Hagar in similar circumstances. It is noteworthy that Ishmael, the product of this union, became the forerunner of a people outside the stream of God's ultimate purposes.

The Apostle Paul used the story of Hagar as an allegory to show how the bondwoman's son represented the Law and its bondage in contrast with Isaac the son of the free woman, who was born later, and is typical of the free-born sons of God enjoying liberty in the church (Galatians 4).

Evidently such unions were not formed in accordance with the will and purpose of God. It is fitting to state, as we write, that this kind of arrangement is already causing deep concern in our society, not only on the part of believers who desire to obey the word of God, but also of responsible legislators, who see the dangers of such mercenary plans becoming yet another threat to family life. The scripture encourages us to pray for such.

Rachel's action therefore savours of expediency, a process by which the counsels of God are set aside for the traditions and ways of men. Her first recourse would have been to invoke the promises of God to Abram. 'Look now toward heaven, and tell the stars, if thou be able to number them; and he said unto him, So shall thy seed be' (Genesis 15:5). The fact that Sarai ignored this promise left no excuse for Rachel to follow her bad example, especially as an even more detailed promise had been made to the patriarch later (Genesis 22:17). Unlike Abram who 'believed God and it was counted unto him for righteousness'; both women forfeited a blessing by not accepting that God may delay the fulfilment of his promises, but never rescinds them. The hopes of both Israel and the church are based on this fact.

Had Rachel acknowledged that the promises of God are inviolate she would have taken the next step and laid the matter before God as Hannah did at a later time when faced with precisely the same problem, for, 'Peninnah had children, but Hannah had no children'; and so, Hannah made a vow saying, 'O Lord of hosts if thou wilt indeed look on the affliction of thine handmaid, and remember me, and not forget thine handmaid, but wilt give unto thine handmaid a man child, then I will give him unto the Lord' (1 Samuel 1:2, 11). Her prayer was answered; she kept her vow, and became the proud mother of the great prophet Samuel.

In setting aside God's promises, and stooping to the folly of expediency, Rachel was typical of Israel in its apostasy. From the time of their emerging as a nation, following the Exodus; Moses had suffered their rebellion, discontent and idolatry. This pattern of behaviour continued during the time of the Judges and later of the Kings; God, with undeserved forbearance, had sent prophets, courageous men who sought to bring about repentance and recovery to the nation; all to no avail. The last and greatest of the prophets, John the Baptist, was executed by command of the puppet Jewish ruler, Herod Antipas, on a sensual festive occasion; and the Saviour came forth as God's last word to the stubborn rebellious nation (Hebrews 1:2).

The time of the nation's rejection of the Saviour, from which there was no turning back, was at the council of Pharisees and high priests which met a few days before the crucifixion, and finally plotted the Lord's death.

'What do we?' they said, 'If we let him thus alone all men will believe on him: and the Romans shall come and take away both our place and nation.' To which Caiaphas, the reigning high priest, replied,

'Ye know nothing at all. Nor consider that it is expedient for us, that one man should die for the people, and the whole nation perish not. And this spake he not of himself; but being high priest that year, he prophesied that Jesus should die for that nation: and not for that nation only, but that also he should gather together in one the children of God that were scattered abroad. *Then from that day forth they took counsel together for to put Him to death*' (John 11:47-53).

Whenever a man sinned more against the light than at that time it would be hard to discover. 'Expediency', to use the chief priest's word, had taken over, and Christ must go to His death.

> 'His (Caiaphas') attitude is determined not by truth of a doctrine, but its effect on the church and the place he and his followers hold in it. What is the word that marks this in the case of every ecclesiastic? You have it here in the life of Caiaphas. It is the word 'expedient'. This word expedient has its time and uses. There are things morally indifferent and the only question is their expediency. But in regard to truth; in regard to questions of the spiritual life and of eternal destiny, the word expedient should never be breathed.'
>
> William Clow *The Day of the Cross* p.20.

Our Lord had foreseen the decision and its fatal outcome as he spake the parable of the Wicked Husbandmen.

> 'A certain man planted a vineyard...and let it

out to husbandmen and went into a far country. And at the season he sent to the husbandmen a servant, that he might receive from the husbandmen of the fruit of the vineyard. And they caught him, and beat him, and sent him away empty. And again he sent another; and him they killed, and many others; beating some, and killing some. Having yet therefore one son, his wellbeloved, he sent him also last unto them, saying, They will reverence my son. But those husbandmen said among themselves, This is the heir; come, let us kill him, and the inheritance shall be ours. And they took him, and killed him, and cast him out of the vineyard. What shall therefore the lord of the vineyard do? *he will come and destroy the husbandmen,* and will give the vineyard unto others (Mark 12:1-3,5-9).

If the Lord's rejection was a final decision, the divine retribution in response was certain, as we learn how true was his prophecy as he was being led to Calvary, amid the wailing women. 'Daughters of Jerusalem', he said, 'weep not for me, but weep for yourselves, and for your children. For, behold, the days are coming, in the which they shall say, Blessed are the barren, and the wombs that never bare, and the paps which never gave suck. Then shall they begin to say to the mountains, Fall on us; and to the hills, Cover us (Luke 23:28-30).

The book of Acts closes its pages before the destruction of Jerusalem occurred but secular history from the pens of Josephus and others tell of the increasing pressure the Jews were effectively applying against the Roman occupiers until Titus brought his armies against Jerusalem in the year AD 70 for the final assault. After stubborn resistance by the Jews, the Romans succeeded in taking Jerusalem, and destroying the temple by fire:—

> Titus ordered that the sanctuary be spared, but the infuriated soldiers refused to listen. A burning torch was hurled through the Golden window, and immediately the wooden beams caught fire. Into the courts the soldiers dashed massacring the thousands who had taken refuge there.
>
> Lewis Browne *The Story of the Jews* p.130.

The Psalmist had prophesied this event in minute detail in these words, 'But now they break down the carved work thereof at once with axes and hammers. They have cast fire into thy sanctuary, they have defiled *by casting down* the dwelling place of thy house to the ground. They said in their hearts, Let us destroy them together, they have burned up all the synagogues of God in the land' (Psalm 74:6-8).

The prophetic words of Rachel at the birth of Dan were fulfilled as she said 'God hath judged me' ... Therefore she called his name Dan (Genesis 30:6).

8

Naphthali — Israel, the Wrestler

'I will scatter you' (Leviticus 26:33; Luke 21:24).

At the same time as Rachel's surrogate son was
born to Bilhah, she exclaimed in apparent triumph,
'With great wrestlings have I wrestled with my
sister, and have prevailed': and she called his name
Naphtali (Wrestling) (Genesis 30:8).

If we take note of the exact circumstances of this
birth, regarding it as a prophetical picture, it is
possible to reach a certain conclusion, as to the
merits, or otherwise, of any conflict which may
have arisen between apostate Israel and the church,
during the present dispensation in spite of certain
erroneous judgments on the part of secular
historians. The details of the story point to Rachel
as the jealous schemer, with Leah adopting a more
passive role.

In contrast with the picture set forth by Dan, of
God's judgment upon Israel at the destruction of
Jerusalem, a direct result of their rejection of the
Saviour, Naphtali (the Wrestler), suggests Israel
endeavouring to stem the tide of those who were
persuaded to follow Christ by the preaching of the
Gospel. Even during our Lord's day the priests and
Pharisees expressed their foreboding when they
said, 'If we let Him thus alone, all men will believe
on Him' (John 11:48).

After Pentecost hostility intensified and as Peter spake with evident conviction of the death and resurrection of the Lord, he prompted them to say 'Men *and* brethren, what shall we do?' (Acts 2:37; cf. 4:16). Frustration on Israel's part led to threatening the apostles as they bore witness (4:17, 21, 29). Soon followed summary imprisonment (5:18), and lastly beatings (5:40).

Finally Stephen was falsely accused before the Sanhedrin and condemned to death by stoning, as the first martyr of the church; as Paul wrote, 'through their fall, salvation *is come* unto the Gentiles, *for to provoke them to jealousy*' (Romans 11:11).

This persecution intensified under the fanatical activities of Saul of Tarsus, whose singular conversion to the faith he had sought to destroy, enabled him to say, later, 'When we were enemies, we were reconciled to God by the death of his Son' (Romans 5:10). From that time, as Paul the apostle of the Gentiles, he boldly witnessed to Israel at great cost to himself. On one occasion he recounted his experiences; 'Of the Jews five times received I forty *stripes* save one. Thrice was I beaten with rods, once I was stoned' (2 Corinthians 1:24-25). Having testified 'to the Jew first', because of their rejection of the Gospel he at last turned from them to the Gentiles in accordance with a prophecy quoted by James; 'Simeon,' he said, 'hath declared how God at the first did visit the Gentiles, to take out of them a people for his name. And to this agree the words of the prophets: as it is written, After this I will return, and will build again the tabernacle of David, which is fallen down; and I will build again the ruins thereof, and will set it up: That the residue of men might seek the Lord, and all the Gentiles, upon whom my name is called' (Acts 15:14-17).

It can be truly stated that there is no record in any part of the Book of the Acts where any Christian believer retaliated physically against his Jewish persecutors. Their only conflict with their rulers was due to the insistence that in preaching the gospel they had to 'obey God rather than man.'

This has been equally true of Christians who rightly interpret the truth concerning Israel in later years. Alas, historians have often confused Christian believers with Christendom, and record the sufferings of Jews, at the hands of Rome for instance, during such times as the Spanish Inquisition! Mention has also been made of men like Luther and Cromwell who, it is alleged, were opposed to the Jews for their failure to embrace the Christian faith. It needs only to be pointed out that whilst the Reformation brought much enlightenment on many facets of Christian doctrine and practice, Protestantism, a by-product of the Reformation, but not to be confused with it, has often 'fallen short' in its protestations rather than declare its affirmations. Present day examples of this come readily to mind!

The fact remains that the Jews have never known truer friends than Christian believers who claim to love and obey God's Word. The many missions to Israel which have been established over the years testify to the truth of this statement.

II

A second fact concerning estranged Israel which is widely acknowledged is her worldwide dispersion which followed the sacking of Jerusalem and the destruction of Herod's temple.

This is seen to be quite distinct in character from the earlier captivities to Assyria and Babylon, at the termination of which a minority of the people returned to a desolate city and no temple. The Diaspora, as it is termed, was the subject of prophecy in many Old Testament Scriptures, and instead of eventually being identified with the host nations as many emigrants do, the Jews managed to retain their national identity. Historians attribute this to their religion, but whilst this may be true to some extent, the undeniable fact is that God has preserved them for future blessing in fulfilment of his ancient promises. The dispersion was not enforced without numerous warnings from the prophets of Israel, that if the nation persisted in its idolatry, and disobedience to God's word, such a catastrophe would occur. Reference to a few of such prophecies which often include details of their final return to Israel for Millennial blessings are given here.

Isaiah 11:11-12 gives details of the godly remnant of the nation being gathered from 'Assyria and from Egypt, and from Pathros and from Cush, and from Elam and from Shinar, and from Hamath, and from the islands of the sea,' and 'Gather together the dispersed of Judah from the four corners of the earth'.

The complete fulfilment of these prophecies will take place when 'all the tribes of the earth mourn, and they shall see the Son of Man coming in the clouds of heaven with power and great glory' (Matthew 24:30-31; Ezekiel 22:15-22). Migration to the State of Israel since it was formed is a 'sign of the times'. The problem of Jews refused exit from behind the Iron Curtain will be resolved at this long-awaited time.

Isaiah 43:5-6 describes the vast extent of this dispersion. 'I will bring my seed from the east, and gather them from the west: I will say to the north, Give up: and to the south, Keep not back: bring my sons from far, and my daughters from the ends of the earth.'

Jeremiah 16:14-21 is couched in similar terms and concludes with the promise 'and they shall know my name is Jehovah' at their return.

Jeremiah 23:3-6 (NIV) speaks of their restoration to prosperity and blessing with the Lord's shepherd care, adding 'nor will any be missing'. David, a Righteous Branch, a King, will be raised up, dispensing justice, and 'Judah will be saved and Israel will live in safety...He will be called The Lord our Righteousness.'

Jeremiah 32:37-44 is of particular comfort to the Jewish remnant, and will repay careful reading.

Jeremiah 50:4-5 speaks of the nation's return in

repentance to enjoy 'a perpetual covenant'.

Amos 9:11-15 prophesies their return to Jerusalem finally restored, unceasing prosperity in the land, 'and they shall no more be pulled up out of their land which I have given them'.

It seems quite clear that these prophecies cannot be applied in any way to the church, since they are concerned with *earthly* blessings.

It has been thought preferable to quote these prophecies of the dispersion, rather than details of the actual movements among the nations, for the sake of space; but interested readers may wish to refer to a history of the Jews, such as Lewis Browne's *Story of the Jews*, published some years ago by Jonathan Cape, but written from the Jewish viewpoint.

The writer describes how the nation sought refuge in Babylon, which was beyond the boundaries of the Roman Empire, after the fall of Jerusalem in the year AD 70. They were relatively secure there until the 8th century (AD 750), when Islam spread to the Fertile Crescent; and persecution drove them to such places as Spain, added to which Rome at the time of the Inquisition in the sixteenth century, also made life intolerable for the Jews; since both Islam and the Roman church tolerated none who were not prepared to become proselytes to their faiths. Large numbers then sought refuge in Poland and neighbouring States where they remained until the present century. These were the main movements but always there were the smaller immigrations, and up to the end of the 18th century Europe made life very difficult for many Jews, and segregated them in ghettoes. Old Jewry in London, derived its name from that time. Later more toleration began to be shown, and from the 19th century life became easier and many settled in all parts of Europe and America, taking part in all aspects of national life in the host countries. The present century has seen dramatic changes. The First World War brought about the end of Turkish rule in Palestine, and the Balfour Declaration in 1917 allowed any Jew who was able to do so, to settle in the land. The Second World War saw Jewish persecution on a massive scale, and the founding of the State of Israel in 1948 did more to bring about the return of Jews to their promised land, in fulfilment of the ancient prophetic Scriptures than at any other time in history. The movement still continues. The recent famine in North Africa has driven another 9000 of the Falasha Jews to their homeland.

III

So far no mention has been made of the moral condition of Israel during the present dispensation, apart from its hostility to the early church.

It will be recalled that our Lord exposed Jewish casuistry for its legalism at the expense of truth. His main charge against them being that they set aside the Word of God by substituting Rabbinic traditions.

In the Gospel by Matthew chapter 23, He summarises much that He had condemned in the earlier years of His ministry. Verses 1-12 warned His hearers against the ostentation and assumed authority seen in both scribes and Pharisees, with the comment that, 'One is your Master, *even* Christ' (v.10).

From verses 13 to 33 He cautioned His followers about their hypocrisy, 'the leaven of the Pharisees and Sadducees,' He termed it. Elsewhere, they were 'blind guides' and their likeness to 'serpents and vipers' described the satanic origins of their evil influence. He would have gathered them to Himself, but their rejection of the prophets, and now of Himself, brought about a state of finality which would end only when, as a repentant nation, they welcomed him as their Messiah in fulfilment of Psalm 118, with the words, 'Blessed is he that cometh in the name of the Lord', to which we have already referred.

The apostasy which our Lord so roundly condemned, not only continued into the present dispensation, but even deepened, in spite of His warnings. As the Jews mourned their plight in Babylon, their one desire was to retain inviolate their religious tradition, as the only means by which their national identity could be assured. Unfortunately, instead of insisting on the Pentateuch being their sole guide, they decided that new circumstances called for new methods, and the Law of Moses with its alleged 613 legal decisions must give place to the Rabbinic Mishna containing 4000 such rules.

But worse was to follow, since 300 years later tradition had fed on itself to such an extent that a new work was compiled which both included and extended the Mishna to 8000 printed pages under 63 headings. This was called the Babylonian Talmud. There is a much condensed version in *Dent's Everyman's Library* edited by Dr A Cohen, containing a mere 400 pages, but sufficient to convey the idea expressed by Paul, that, 'blindness in part is happened to Israel' (Romans 11:25). As Lewis Browne admits, 'the Jews lifted it to a place of importance above the very Bible.' It was no longer a thing to live *by* but a thing to live *for*. Speaking to a Hebrew Christian friend some years ago about the oddities of the Talmud, he remarked, 'Yes, I admit there are some strange things in the Talmud, but I consider that some of the traditions of the Church are far worse'; a cautionary statement we do well to ponder!

In spite of this, some orthodox Jews are turning to the Scriptures and some even reading the New Testament, though the results are so far not extensive. As encouraging as this may be, we must expect the Church to grow mainly from Gentile sources, 'until the fulness of the Gentiles be come in' (Romans 11:25). This verse indicates two vital moments in God's prophetic programme, (1) this 'fulness of the Gentiles' coincides with the completion of the church at the 'coming of the Lord', and (2) the moment when He will once more take up the cause of His ancient people of Israel. Their prospect at first will indeed be grim, as His prophetic warning of the 'usurper' will be literally fulfilled, 'I am come in my Father's name, and ye receive me not; if another shall come in his own name, him ye will receive' (John 5:43).

Apart from a minority, the godly remnant of Israel, which will be awaiting the coming of the true Messiah (Luke 21:28), the rest of the nation will suffer a major crisis, a self-inflicted judgment which will decimate the numbers, leaving the remnant to welcome its Redeemer, with evidences of repentance and ultimate joy (Isaiah 66:5).

Further details of this are reserved for a later chapter.

9

Gad — the Rebel Troop

'The Kingdom of heaven is like a grain of mustard seed...when it was grown...it becometh a tree, so that the birds of the air come and lodge in the branches thereof' (Matthew 13:31-32).

Contrary to what might have been expected, following the first impact of the church, with all the blessings suggested by the names of the first four sons of Leah, regrettably this early promise was not sustained; not that the blessings ceased, but the time came when rapid growth continued at the expense of spirituality, and influence in society.

Such a situation was foreshadowed in the continuing story of Leah. After the first sons were born, and Rachel bore two sons, in name only, by surrogation, Leah's and Jacob's early satisfaction seems to have diminished as Leah had become barren, and desired further sons.

If Rachel's plan had worked, why not follow her example? Regardless of God's will in the matter, she too gave her handmaid Zilpah to Jacob and expediency seemed to work once more! At the time of her son's birth she exclaimed, 'A troop cometh', and she called his name Gad' (Genesis 30:11). Leah's family had increased but at a cost to be seen in later years. Isaiah seems to have described the situation, 'Thou hast multiplied the nation, and not increased the joy' (Isaiah 9:3).

Our Lord's parable of the mustard tree (quoted above) tells also of phenomenal growth contrary to the laws of nature. Mustard might be 'the greatest among herbs' but in the instance cited, 'it becometh a tree, so that the birds of the air lodge in its branches.'

We may well ask why these 'Kingdom parables' of Matthew (ch 13) have elements of good and bad in the various situations. As the sower casts forth his seed, hard behind him, 'The fowls come and devour them up', but here the birds are lodging in the branches of the mustard tree. What first appeared as robbers to be scared away, are now appearing as lodgers in the branches of the tree.

This 'mystery of the Kingdom' cannot represent the church of God as He intends it to be, but rather Christendom as we know it, which contains what is of God, but suffers serious adulteration by doctrines and practices introduced like the sons of the bondwomen, as a result of worldly wisdom.

In every work of God, He abhors mixtures of the sacred and profane. The principle is stated clearly in the law of Moses; the horse and ass were not to be yoked together; clothes were not to be made of differing yarns, and in the typical service of God, altars of stone and earth were not to be built by the would-be worshipper.

One of the severest trials befell the people of Israel on the occasion when 'the *mixt multitude* that *was* among them fell a lusting' (Numbers 11:4). Instead of manna, the heaven-sent food, they desired flesh and the breath-contaminating foods of Egypt. The unspiritual have little desire for the Living Bread, 'the flesh' has a very different appetite. Little wonder that God's judgment fell upon them, 'while their meat *was* yet in their mouths, the wrath of God çame upon them, and slew the fattest of them' (Psalm 78:30-31).

The New Testament writers warned of such a development in the professing church in very plain words. Paul wrote of a 'falling away' before the onset of the coming 'day of Christ' (2 Thessalonians 2:3). The term, 'falling away' is translated from the Greek *APOSTASIA* from which we derive the word "apostasy". *Cassells' Dictionary of Religion* gives the following meaning of the word:

> 'This word in the original signifies the desertion or standing away by a soldier from the commander and cause, to whom, and to which, he has promised allegiance. It was adapted for Christians as a designation for the forsaking of Christianity, those giving up their faith being called 'apostates'.'

Making a distinction between his own age and our own Paul wrote, 'Now the Spirit speaketh expressly, that in the *latter times*, some shall depart from the faith, giving heed to seducing spirits, and doctrines of devils' (1 Timothy 4:1). He also warned that 'in the *last days*' men would 'have a form of godliness, but denying the power thereof.' (2 Timothy 3:1, 5)

Peter also wrote, 'there shall come in the *last days*, scoffers, walking after their own lusts, And saying, Where is the promise of His coming? for since the fathers fell asleep, all things continue as *they were* from the beginning of creation' (2 Peter 3:3, 4). Is Peter thinking of a minority? Alas, no, for he writes, *'many* shall follow their pernicious ways: by reason of whom the way of truth shall be evil spoken of' (2 Peter 2:2). It would seem that by a gradual process of accretion, changes are taking place, of which the masses of Christendom are unaware.

The oldest surviving historic church is the vast Roman Catholic system. It adheres to some truth that is according to Scripture, and in many ways more rigidly than the 'free churches' of Christendom, but it also embraces much more that has no such authority; it claims that the church is the final authority by the specious argument that it existed before the canon of Scripture was complete. In all this it is a notable example of our contention. We have culled the following passage from Mr George Goodman's small book, *The Gospel we Preach*. He tells of an experience of his during a visit abroad.

'I stood once in the Roman Catholic Cathedral in Vienna. Mass was being celebrated, the altar was ablaze with candles, and at it knelt a priest in gorgeous robes; before him on the altar was a wafer of bread which he adored on his knees with every gesture of zealous devotion. As he did so he repeated some Latin sentences while the people stood or sat around in an irregular group and chanted a dirge-like hymn. In other parts of the building some knelt and told their beads before the images of the virgin or of their favourite saint, only indirectly interested in what was going on.

'As I contemplated the scene the question rose in me: "Is this christianity? Is this in accord with the new life and simplicity that is in Christ?" No, it bore no resemblance to it. Whatever may be said for it, one could not but recognise that it breathed an entirely different spirit from that in which one lives and moves and has his being when he opens the New Testament. There was something radically different, the growth of years of perversion and accretion.

'The original thing of beauty, simplicity, and liberty had entirely disappeared. What remains is 'another gospel' which is not another (Galatians 1:8; 2 Corinthians 11:4). One feels that the 'Jesus' who is supposed to be present in the wafer adored is 'another Jesus' (2 Corinthians 11:4) whom the apostles have not preached, so that the whole is permeated with 'another spirit' and not with the Holy Spirit of truth which the true christian has received.

'That all this priestcraft should be presented to the onlookers instead of the 'truth which is in Jesus' is lamentable. It is giving those who ask for bread, a stone.

'I once asked a priest who had come into the light of the Gospel, if those who did such things in the name of Christ did not hold the doctrines of grace, of free and full salvation by faith in Jesus? Were they ignorant of them, or did they not believe them? His reply was suggestive, 'Yes!' he said, 'we professed to hold them all, but they were buried in rubbish'. Alas, that it should be so!

'One searches the New Testament in vain for any evidence or suggestion of the gorgeous organisation of Rome, of its prelates and priests, its clerics and its ritual and ordinances. Yet these are prominent things which have obscured the truth and darkened the true light that shines in the Gospel, which is 'the power of God unto salvation to everyone that believeth.'

'And what is true of the sad apostasy of Rome, is also true in measure of her daughters. For she is the 'Mother of Harlots'.'

Those readers from an earlier generation who were privileged to know this writer well, will be fully aware that whilst he held such critical views about the Papal system, he would have freely encouraged any who, as individuals, sought release from its baneful teachings and influences. This would have applied to those who experienced for the first time the joy of conversion to Christ, or those already believers within the system seeking a more scriptural form of worship and service outside its fold. Such a decision is one of extreme urgency in view of signs indicating Christ's imminent return, and holds good for those in every other apostate faith or cult.

Looking at the various Christian Confessions apart from Rome we discover similar growth, albeit in the aggregate rather than in any one organisation, but having no common scriptural basis of doctrine, with resulting confusion. The best that has been advocated as a suggested remedy to the chaos is an all-inclusive union which ignores the causes of division.

The Ecumenical Movement fostered by the World Council of Churches is not content with seeking union with Rome, but like Rome itself, has no hesitation in joining forces increasingly with a wide spread of non-Christian faiths, in face of Scripture's complete condemnation of such approaches. In the W.C.C's exhaustive reports but few Scriptures are quoted, and these assumed to support their aims. It seems to have been forgotten that the Christian faith is dogmatic in the highest sense in that it sees God as sole Creator; Christ as man's only Redeemer, and offers man no hope of salvation outside Himself. He Himself said, 'I am the way, the truth, and the life: no man cometh unto the Father but by me' (John 14:6). Peter, speaking at Pentecost, also said, 'Neither is there salvation in any other; for there is none other name under heaven given among men, whereby we must be saved' (Acts 4:12).

Furthermore, Paul writing to Timothy declares, '*there is* one God, and one mediator between God and men, the man Christ Jesus; who gave himself a ransom for all' (1 Timothy 2:5-6).

During the long history of the church revivals have occurred at intervening periods, when after confession and repentance on the part of its members, the Spirit of God has brought about a new commitment to God and His cause. The Reformation period and the Evangelical revivals of the eighteenth and nineteenth centuries are notable examples of such, when faith, once discarded, was recovered, and the faith and practices of the early church once more enjoyed.

It may not be too late for another revival, even a greater one! Past revivals have been for the most part but partial. What is now required is a bold step of faith; it may be costly in these days of extreme reactions; costly too as the people of God acknowledge in repentance and confession past failure to accept the Lordship of Christ, and live in obedience to His Word. It would be a welcome change if, instead of exhausting themselves trying to work for God in their own way, Christians followed the Apostolic example and implored God to work through and with His people (Acts 14:27, 15:4, 12).

Apart from such a revival, which can take place in the brief time which may be granted to the church before the coming of the Lord, Christendom will after that event continue its headstrong course and destiny, to which we will return later.

10

Asher — Insecure Satisfaction

'Thou sayest, I am rich and increased with goods and have need of nothing' (Revelation 3:17; 17:2-6).

The birth of Asher, the last of the surrogate sons of Jacob, was hailed by a further excited cry from Leah, *'Happy* am I, for the daughters will call me *blessed,* and she called his name Asher' (Genesis 30:13 AV). That the last son among the surrogates should bear a name which will be seen to describe the boasted claims of the Laodicean church during the last days of the Christian era is, in itself, significant.

Happiness and joy are distinctly separate emotions. The Oxford English Dictionary definition of 'Happy' (of persons or circumstances) 'lucky, fortunate, contented or pleased with one's lot, successful, apt, felicitous' is a very different concept than that of Christian joy, a positive aspect of blessedness defined by our Lord, as He described the fruitful vine to be symbolic of Himself and His faithful followers (John 15:11; also 1 John 1:4; 2 John 12; 3 John 4).

The 'happiness' of Leah was based on the insecure foundation of an unholy relationship. Admittedly the word 'happiness' has many other occurrences in Scripture which describe a healthy situation, but often it is based on good fortune

(Psalm 127:5), or satisfaction, even when an act of treachery has been committed (Jeremiah 12:1). There was an occasion when Israel's faith was at low ebb and God accused His people, 'Ye have said it is vain to serve God', and, 'ye call the proud happy' (Malachi 3:14-15).

The last days of Christendom, even now with us, will increasingly be marked by the professing church in the majority of cases having lost their sense of vocation to proclaim the Gospel. Political and social matters will more than ever dominate its aims. To quote Paul's letter to Timothy, there will be those who are 'lovers of pleasures more than lovers of God; Having a form of godliness, but denying the power thereof: *from such turn away*' (2 Timothy 3:4-5). Such is the tragic prophetic picture of Laodicea the apostate church.

We believe that the time-honoured interpretation by devout scholars such as Walter Scott and John Ashton Savage, of the spiritual state of each of the seven churches of Asia in turn, affords an illustration of the consecutive history of the church during this age, and still holds good (Revelation chs. 2 and 3).

The usual pattern is as follows:

Ephesus	—First century conditions
Smyrna	—Persecution and martyrdom, (Second and third centuries)
Pergamos	—Union of Church and State during the reign of Emperor Constantine, evidences of which still remain.
Thyatira	—The age dominated by early Catholi-

cism, and still a great religious power.

Sardis —The period of the early reformed churches, including the Protestant off-shoot, dated from the 16th and 17th centuries.

Philadelphia—Revival time in the 19th century, when for a few years much neglected truth was recovered.

Laodicea —Descriptive of the present day. Its apostate character leaves no room for any misunderstanding on the part of those willing to recognise the facts.

The three churches, Thyatira, Sardis and Philadelphia are each seen to be spiritually represented at the time of the Lord's second coming according to the following statements:

To Thyatira —'Hold fast till I come' (Revelation 2:25).

To Sardis —'Thou shalt not know what hour I shall come upon thee' (3:3).

To Philadelphia—'Behold I come quickly: hold that fast which thou hast' (3:11).

No such exhortation is given to Laodicea, as a church, though individuals are promised a blessing from its ranks, as we shall see later. The reference to Christ's coming to Ephesus, (2:3), is of a judicial nature, warning the church of its need for repentance as a condition to save its extinction, otherwise it was warned its candlestick of witness would be removed.

The differences between the Laodicean church

and its three predecessors call for a special examination as to its character and destiny. Although these churches run parallel in time with Laodicea and each have an independent historical background, yet simultaneously they share the failure of apostasy to a greater or lesser degree but it is the Laodicean church which the Spirit of God has named to illustrate the 'falling away' on behalf of the rest, as she boasts of her dubious wealth, with self complacency.

II

The acquisition of wealth for its own sake and for its supposed advantages, usually described as materialism, is no new phenomenon. As far back in history as Jeremiah's day, the prophet could write, 'Let not the rich *man* glory in his riches: But let him that glorieth glory in this, that he understandeth and knoweth me, that I *am* the Lord which exercise loving-kindness, judgment, and righteousness, in the earth; for in these *things* I delight, saith the Lord' (Jeremiah 9:23-24).

Paul too taunted the Corinthian believers, 'now ave reigned as kings without us: and I would to God ye ye are rich, ye hdid reign' (1 Corinthians 4:8). James too made some severe criticisms of those who 'heaped up treasure together for the last days' (James 5:3).

As Christ addresses the angel of the church to Laodicea, He introduces Himself as the Amen, the faithful and true witness (Revelation 3:14). It may be of help to newcomers to the study of the

Scriptures to point out that the title AMEN is derived from the Hebrew word *AMETH*, for *truth** and the appellation 'the faithful and true witness' is a fitting description of the One who could claim that He embodied truth in Himself (John 14:6). He tells this church in common with the others, 'I know thy works' and the notable feature which marks His firm attitude toward all the churches is His impartial judgment; the One who is taking account of each company of believers in every age.

Walter Scott commenting on this title makes the following impassioned statement:

> 'Every witness for God, individual and corporate, has failed save One. The church so *richly endowed* with truth and privilege is the worst offender of any of the witnessing company from Adam downwards. Has it been a faithful custodian of Divine grace? Is it a true witness to the character of God? Is it the living expression on earth of Jesus Christ of what He was and is? Alas, no!! The church has shut Him out. Hear its jubilant strain, 'I am rich and increased in goods, and have need of nothing!' Not even of Christ, the church's life and glory! He thus is driven out yet lingers about the door, taking His stand outside. 'Behold' this wonder of wonders, 'I stand at the door and knock'

*In Isaiah 65:16 we have this statement, 'He that blesseth himself in the earth shall bless himself in the God of truth.' The word in Hebrew for TRUTH, used twice in this verse, is AMEN.

and such is His attitude today. The church is the most responsible witness which has ever appeared, and is now a huge wreck. It is being morally ruined, not by open enemies, but by professed friends. Boastful, proud, loaded with wealth and content, while Christ is outside! Such was Laodicea and such is the church today. She has been neither a faithful or true witness but Christ is, and thus once again 'the heart is relieved as it turns from the wreck and ruin around Him'.'

Exposition of the Book of Revelation pp.109-110.

Laodicea was a church Paul had special care for some years earlier as he wrote to the Colossians, 'I want you to know how much I am struggling for you and for those at Laodicea...that they may be encouraged in heart and united in love, so that they may have the *full riches* of complete understanding, in order that they may know the mystery of God, namely Christ, in whom are hidden *all the treasures* of wisdom and knowledge' (Colossians 2:1-2 NIV Revised Ed.). Alas, Paul's desire that they might have these heavenly treasures was soon forgotten as the years of decline took their toll.

Having scrutinised Laodicea at the time of His approach, the Lord makes His assessment of her true state. His first comment is that 'thou art lukewarm, and neither cold nor hot' (Revelation 3:16). She is in a lethargic condition in which she neither cheers by the radiation of her warmth, nor is she stimulated into action by her coldness. She just drifts along with the stream, refusing to fight or protest except in matters which are manifestly outside her true sphere, be they political or social, a legacy from the days which we have already remarked, when church and State formed a union which could only be to the detriment of the former's witness. Power and influence in world affairs has become her ambition, and luxury and ease her rewards. Apostate Laodicea is only fit to be figuratively vomited from the Lord's mouth; soul-winning is no longer her true vocation!

As the Lord makes His appraisal of her, He applies the same values in His judgment as He did many years earlier at the time of David's anointing to Israel's kingship by Samuel, '*the Lord seeth* not as man seeth; for man looketh on the outward appearance, but the Lord looketh on the heart' (1 Samuel 16:7). Outwardly Laodicea, as she was then, and is today in her figurative role, has much to commend her in the estimation of the worldly-wise; a well organised body, controlled by men of fine intellect and patronised by the influential people of the day, she is endowed with vast material wealth, and represented by edifices which are admired by millions. Her standing in society ensures that she is consulted on all kinds of social, legislative and ethical problems, and, when she is not referred to, is all too ready to proffer her advice, controversial or otherwise. In the Lord's sight however, her health has much to be desired as He briefly pronounces 'thou art wretched, and miserable, and poor, and blind, and naked' (Revelation 3:17).

'Wretched'—the Lord makes use of the same word as did Paul as he saw himself as a believer conflicting with the bondage of the law of sin, saying, 'O wretched man that I am! who shall deliver me from the body of this death?' (Romans 7:24).

Unlike the Apostle, Laodicea cannot bring herself to confess her morbid condition, and find deliverance like Paul, in the liberty of the Spirit.

In similar vein the Lord speaks of the church as 'miserable' and using another example from Paul's Epistles we read 'If in this life only we have hope in Christ we are of all men most *miserable*' (1 Corinthians 15:19). Pre-occupation with life's comforts is a poor substitute for the place, where we can say, in the words of the Messianic Psalm, 'in thy presence *is* fulness of joy; at thy right hand *there are* pleasures for evermore' (Psalm 16:11). Beside the hope of resurrection there is the increasing imminence of the 'blessed hope' of Christ's return!

In spite of Laodicea's claim, 'I am rich', the Lord spake otherwise; she was 'poor'; the same word as the Lord used to describe the poor widow, (Luke 21:3) who had little of material wealth, but in His sight 'cast in more than they all'. Like the rich fool of Luke 12, it can be said of them, 'So *is* (she) that layeth up treasure for (herself) and is not rich toward God' (v.21).

Blindness—spiritual blindness—was her next problem, a judicial blindness which was self-inflicted. Isaiah bore a similar message to Israel from God. 'Go tell this people...see ye indeed, and perceive not...and shut their eyes; lest they see' (Isaiah 6:9-10). Of the Pharisees the Lord said, 'Ye say 'We see'; therefore your sin remaineth' (John

9:39-41).

Finally the penetrating eyes of the Lord discovered the 'nakedness' of the Laodiceans; the 'robe of righteousness' was missing, if indeed it had ever been donned!

But the Lord never leaves His professed church in this state without offering some means of recovery and says to Laodicea, 'Buy of me...white raiment, that thou mayest be clothed, and that the shame of thy nakedness do not appear' (Revelation 3:19). Nothing that the Laodicean church can do will remedy this condition, the imputed righteousness which Christ alone provides is her only hope. Says Paul, 'put off your old self, which is being corrupted by its deceitful desires; to be made new in the attitude of your minds; and to *put on* the new self created to be like God in true righteousness and holiness' (Ephesians 4:22-23 NIV).

F W Pitt writing of the man who was given a place of privilege because of his 'goodly apparel' (James 2:2) makes the following comment:

'A man may wear humble clothes, and yet be the possessor of a most attractive wardrobe for the soul, the 'robe of righteousness' that Isaiah 56:10 speaks of may be his, the 'garment of praise' in the 3rd verse of the same chapter may be given him by his Lord—it is a lovely dress. 'Be clothed with humility' says 1 Peter 5:5 and that is a sartorial fashion greatly esteemed in the streets of heaven: the 'whole armour of God' so grandly described in Ephesians 6:14-18 occupies a cupboard

all of itself in the soul's dressing room,
and 'above all things put on charity'
Colossians 3:14 reminds us, and that is a
glorious overcoat more warming to the
heart than any fur coat to the body.'
The Belief that Behaves pp.40-41.

The Lord has a remedy too for Laodicea's
poverty, 'I counsel thee to buy of me gold tried in
the fire, that thou mayest be rich' (v.18). Like every
worthwhile spiritual possession it may be bought
'without money and without price'.

The epistle to the Ephesians which treats of the
believer's wealth in chapters 1-3, has more to say
about our heavenly possessions than any other
epistle. In our salvation, 'we have redemption
through his blood, the forgiveness of sins, according
to the *riches of his grace*' (Ephesians 1:7), and again, 'in
the ages to come he might show the exceeding *riches
of his grace* in *his* kindness toward us through Christ
Jesus (Ephesians 2:7). About the word 'grace'
(*charis*), Mr Vine remarks,

'There is stress on its freeness and
universality, its spontaneous character as
in the case of God's redemptive mercy,
and the pleasure or joy He designs for the
recipient'.
Dictionary of New Testament Words p.500 'b'.

Paul in his prayer, asks that the believer 'may
know what is the hope of his calling, and what the
riches of the glory of his inheritance in the saints'
(Ephesians 1:18) compare (1 Peter 1:4).

Closely linked with God's riches of grace are His
'*riches of mercy*' (2:4). If the former speaks of God's

bounty, the latter must describe our extreme need. Mr Vine again:

> 'It is the outward manifestation of pity, it assumes need on the part of him who receives it, and resources. adequate to meet the need on the part of him who shows it' (Ibid p.732).

To the Gentiles, Paul says he was given grace, 'that I should preach among the Gentiles *the unsearchable riches* of Christ' (Ephesians 3:7-8). Laodicea had despised her heritage. In that same prayer he pleads that the Lord Jesus Christ, 'would grant you according *to the riches of his glory*, to be strengthened in might by his Spirit in the inner man' (Ephesians 3:16), 'his manifestation in grace toward believers' (Vine).

Elsewhere Paul tells us that 'for your sakes he became poor, that ye through his poverty *might be rich*' (2 Corinthians 8:9), and commenting on Moses' choice writes, 'Esteeming the reproach of Christ *greater riches* than the treasures of Egypt' (Hebrews 11:26). He seems to hardly constrain himself as he exclaims, 'O the depth of the *riches* both of the wisdom and knowledge of God! how unsearchable *are* his judgments and his ways past finding out' (Romans 11:33).

As F W Pitt remarks:

> 'This wealth is not stored up in any earthly bank. These are treasures in heaven that Matthew 6:20 speaks about. Good deeds done in Christ's Name, earnest prayers, services rendered, souls won, days and powers spent for Him—

these things and others like them, pass
for valuables in that place whose gates are
of pearl, and whose streets are of gold,'
(Ibid pp.44-45).

The remaining invitation the Lord gives to
Laodicea is 'anoint thine eyes with eyesalve, that
thou mayest see' (Revelation 3:18). That which is
undoubtedly our most precious faculty, when loss
causes us greatest distress, and is not without
remedy in its spiritual counterpart. If what has
gone before were taken seriously there would be
little doubt that the repentant apostate's spiritual
perception would pass the test. When the Saviour
gave His well known discourse to the company
gathered in the synagogue at Nazareth, one of the
blessings He promised the willing recipients of His
message, was 'the recovering of sight to the blind'
(Luke 4:18). The inference we may draw from this
promise is that it does not refer exclusively to one
'born blind' but of *recovery* on the part of others who
once saw and whose eyes have been blinded, by the
god of this world, through unbelief.

The attitude of the Lord now changes; He has
diagnosed their ills, and offered effective remedies,
and we have no hint that Laodicea as a church
responded to these overtures. Nevertheless, all is
not lost, for where the body corporate fails, there
remains the appeal to the individual, 'if any man
hear my voice, and open the door, I will come in, and
will sup with him, and he with me' (Revelation
3:20). The long-suffering of the Lord may be seen
by the sequence of steps in His appeal to the erring
Church, first he perceives their state, He then

knocks, waits, and seeks entry to the willing host, that He might join in hallowed communion with such an one. However much we may lament the state of the 20th century Church, the Lord's faithfulness need never be in doubt; as Paul writes to Timothy on the subject of godly order in the Church he makes this comment, 'If we believe not *yet* he abideth faithful; he cannot deny himself' (2 Timothy 2:13). Peter, in the energy of the flesh, could boast, 'If I should die with thee, I will not deny thee in any wise' (Mark 14:31), but it is Christ alone who can promise the constancy of His love, and will never deny those who are responsive to His overtures, even though Laodicea as a body leave Him no alternative to rejection.

This dispensation ends with the final verse of Revelation 3, as the Lord still addressing the individual says, 'He that hath an ear, let him hear what the Spirit saith to the churches' (v.22). These will take part in the translation of the church at the coming of the Lord, and Laodicea in company with all those that are left behind from the various factions of the apostate Church will have to face Divine judgment.

III

When the united restraints of the Holy Spirit and the church of God no longer contain the growth of the apostasy after the church's removal from earth, the situation in Christendom will change speedily and dramatically. We base this prediction on our understanding of Paul's statement, 'And now we know *what* witholdeth, that he (i.e., the man of sin) might be revealed in his time. For the mystery of iniquity doth already work; only *he* that now letteth (restraineth) *will let* until *he* be taken out of the way' (2 Thessalonians 2:7). The words *what* witholdeth and *'he* who now letteth' would therefore refer to the inseparable bond between the church of God and the Holy Spirit in their joint restraining influence before the Lord's coming. There are other interpretations of these verses, but this seems to harmonise with other prophetic scriptures.

Older Christians are impressed by the number of Bible prophecies which have been fulfilled during this twentieth century. At its commencement Islamic Turkey occupied Palestine and was expelled during the 1914-1918 war by the British forces under General Allenby. Following the British Protectorate period, the State of Israel was established in 1948. Since then the settlement of Jews in Israel has gathered pace until today millions have claimed citizenship there, and continue to do so.

Some earlier prophetic students had expected this migration to take place after the translation of the church at the Lord's coming. A writer we have referred to, J A Savage, considered that, according to Zechariah's prophecy, Judah and Benjamin would be the first to return. *Scroll of Time* p.70.

A further development of recent years has been the formation of the World Council of Churches, with its grandiose plans to merge all Christendom, including the Papal church as its senior partner, into one vast union. About the year 1970, discussions began between the major Protestant churches and

Rome to further this end. In 1983 two reports on these talks were published to discover the Church of England's response. One of these was the World Council of Churches B.E.M. report on *Baptism, Eucharist* and *Ministry*, and the other ARCIC *Final Report of the Anglican Roman-Catholic International Commission*. Since then a committee of twenty two members of the Anglican, Faith and Order Group, has met under the chairmanship of the Bishop of Chichester. This has considered the two Reports and, in 1985, produced their own document entitled *Toward a Church of England Response to BEM and ARCIC*.

It seems quite clear from this publication that there is a very positive leaning by the non-Catholic churches toward Rome; ('Paragraph 9' on the effects of the Reformation).

> 'Whatever its positive results it shattered the unity of the Church in the West and introduced the contrast between the traditional structure of the ministry, and the structure which developed from the Reformation, which are among the principal Ecumenical problems of today.'

If pre-Reformation unity is the objective of the churches behind this report, then the only unity envisaged is that owning Papal authority. This trend toward Rome has evidently been welcomed by Dr Runcie, the Archbishop of Canterbury, who has stated that he is prepared to acknowledge the Pontiff of Rome as 'first among equals', whatever that means! A commentator on this latest Report in the radio programme 'Sunday' has suggested that very little has changed; it needs but scant observation to realise that while the non-Catholic churches have been engaged in endless complicated discussions, the Roman church has conceded little or nothing of material importance, and meanwhile has expedited its own ambitious programme for religious supremacy as never before, with the Pope addressing, in all, millions of his followers at impressive stage-managed gatherings on a world-wide scale. (For a more comprehensive assessment of the Ecumenical Movement, see 'Appendix 'C'.)

A further important development during this century has been the formation of the European Economic Community, which under the terms of the Treaty of Rome was ratified in the year 1958 with six nations comprising its nucleus, but excluding Great Britain, one of its main architects. It has since been enlarged with Britain participating as a rather uneasy member. Its aims are to remove all barriers against movements of capital, labour, goods and services, with the prospect of a common currency. Its members claim that experience shows it to be of advantage to international trade though national sovereignty has to be acceded on some points. From the time of the middle ages, prophetic students have expected a multinational revived Roman Empire to emerge after the church's translation, and the Community in its final shape may well fulfil this prediction.

Bearing in mind the two outlined contemporary movements on the religious and political fronts, these may well portend earth-shattering developments unparalleled in all human history. These changes, equated with so-called 'progress', are taking place so rapidly as to pass almost without notice; the masses having become inured to change.

Since our immediate purpose is to treat of the apostasy of the professing church, any reference to prophetic truth must be confined to that subject, and the political considerations only as far as they converge on the first of these. Such a confluence of interests is clearly described in the book of Revelation, and its results will be seen shortly following on the translation of the redeemed to heaven at the coming of the Lord Jesus Christ.

In chapter 17 of this great prophecy, the apostate church is seen as the amalgam of all those who have departed from the faith they once professed; it is called by the unflattering name of 'the Great Whore', and 'The Mother of Harlots' because of her unfaithfulness to Christ and His cause.

Coupled with this title is that of 'Mystery Babylon', possibly an allusion to the confusion inherent in its constituent parts. Her colourful pretentious wealth is but a camouflage for her real character, as her corruption and persecutions even to martyrdom are called to mind. Her patrons are found among royalty and the leaders in commerce who never question, and even admire, her power and influence as she boasts, 'I sit a queen, and am no widow, and shall see no sorrow' (Revelation 18:7).

In the *material* world her patrons deal in precious things of high value, down to the essential commodities of life.

At the *human* level she has complete control over her members' bodies until they can regard themselves as no more than her slaves, and at the *spiritual* level their destiny is in her hands as she traffics in that most precious of all possessions, 'the souls of men' (Revelation 17:11-13).

This is a symbolic picture of her influence at the acme of her power, and how fitting is Solomon's picture of the 'strange woman' (Proverbs 7). Full of religion she says to her clients, 'I have peace offerings with me; this day have I paid my vows...the good man is not at home, he is gone a long journey...and will come home at the time appointed...He goeth after her as an ox to the slaughter...Her house is the way to hell' (vs. 5, 14, 19-20, 22, 27).

This vast system will function with the revived Roman Empire of Western Europe and become the religious partner of that great political union under the satanic character 'The Beast'; and John by the Spirit reveals something of this union in these words, 'I will tell thee the mystery of the woman, *and the beast that carrieth her,* which hath seven heads and ten horns...And the ten horns which thou sawest upon the beast, these shall hate the whore, and shall make her desolate, and naked, and shall eat her flesh, and shall burn her with fire. For God hath put in their hearts to fulfil his will...and give their kingdom unto the beast...And the woman which thou sawest is that great city, which reigneth over the kings of the earth' (Revelation 17:7, 16-18). In this manner will the judgment of God be carried out upon the apostate church, not by direct action on His part but by the agency of the Beast himself, her former associate in the evil confederacy.

The sequel to this judicial retribution of the

apostate church is seen in the mortification of her erstwhile admirers as the kings cry, 'Alas, alas, that great city Babylon, that mighty city! for in one hour is thy judgment come.' In like manner her merchants wail, 'Alas, alas, that great city, that was clothed in fine linen, and purple, and scarlet, and decked with gold, and precious stones, and pearls! in one hour *so great riches* come to nought.' Then the shipmasters, sailors, and traders join in with their laments, 'Alas, alas, that great city, wherein were made rich all that had ships in the sea by reason of her costliness! for in one hour is she made desolate' (Revelation 18:10, 16-17, 19). Finally, after the divine Judge has considered every mitigating circumstance, 'much people in heaven' praise God by saying, 'true and righteous are His judgments: for he hath judged the great whore, which did corrupt the earth with her fornication, and hath avenged the blood of his servants at her hand'. And again they said Alleluia. And her 'smoke rose up for ever and ever' (Revelation 19:1-3). Fittingly, immediately following this is the nuptial day of the bride, the true church of God, 'arrayed in fine linen, clean and white; for the fine linen is the righteousness of saints' (Revelation 19:8).

This solemn appraisal of the growth and ultimate fate of the apostate religious, and the political power of the coming 'Beast', call for a message of hope for those who are prepared to take the bold step of severance from this religious system. It is, 'Come out of her, my people, that ye be not partaker of her sins, and that ye receive not of her plagues' (Revelation 18:4). This means nothing less than withdrawal from the Papal system, and all who come in any way under the aegis of the 'World Council of Churches'; and to search for such gatherings of believers who take the Word of God in all its simplicity for their guide for doctrine and practice.

It is possible that some reader will be convinced of the errors of the apostate church and yet not know the joy which comes with the possession of eternal life. The Lord's last message to the church in Laodicea should be heeded, 'If any man hear my voice, and open the door, I will come in to him, and will sup with him, and he with me' (Revelation 3:20), and again, 'as many as received him to them gave he the power to become the sons of God, *even* to them that believe on his name' (John 1:12). If sin is the barrier, even the sin of unbelief, God's final word must be 'the blood of Jesus Christ his Son cleanseth us from all sin' (1 John 1:7). The church has no power to save; Christ alone is the Saviour, 'him that cometh to me,' He says, 'I will in no wise cast out.' (John 6:37). The 'church' may fail, but Christ, never.

11

Issachar — Hire and Reward

'Judge nothing before the time, until the Lord comes...then shall every man have praise of God' (1 Corinthians 4:5).

We have no better example of a man whose life was spent in service in prospect of reward, than in the case of Jacob himself. In the first instance his recompense was denied him, as he later told his father-in-law Laban: 'I have been twenty years in thy house; I served thee fourteen years for thy two daughters, and six years for thy cattle' (Genesis 31:41). Leah however could not equal the patience of her husband, as we recall his long years of service for the hand of Rachel.

As Leah bore her fifth true son, she attributed his birth to God as a sign of His favour saying, 'God hath given me my hire...and she called his name Issachar' (hire) (Genesis 30:18, margin). Her motive and action may have been wrong, but God mercifully overruled in this, to furnish in Leah an illustration of service and reward, for the church.

The word *HIRE* is seen to have two connotations in scripture; firstly that in common usage when a person is engaged in service for reward; and secondly, as in this instance when 'hire' means the reward itself. In the church both obtain; and for the service that is rendered here and now there will be compensating rewards at the Judgment Seat of Christ. Fortunately, for the Lord's servant, the picture is inappropriate since the hired servant of Hebrew times had no security of tenure as did his counterpart the bond servant. This concept is aptly illustrated in the type of the Hebrew servant of Exodus chapter 21. Firstly, he was purchased by his future master. In those conditions money sufficed to effect the transaction, but the bond servants of Christ are 'not redeemed with corruptible things as silver and gold...but with the precious blood of Christ' (1 Peter 1:18-19) of inestimable worth.

Having been bought, after the prescribed period of six years according to the Law, the bondservant could claim his freedom in the seventh year of his service, and during that time he was, in a restricted sense, both a bondman and a freeman. Paul sees the Lord's servant today in similar light, saying, 'he that is called in the Lord, *being* a servant, is the Lord's free man: likewise also he that is called, *being* free, is Christ's servant' (1 Corinthians 7:22).

In days when such social bondage has been outmoded, it can still be true that in our relationship to our Master we delight in the bond by which we are held, and see it to be one of perfect freedom, as He says, 'Take my yoke upon you, and learn of me; for I am meek and lowly in heart: and ye shall find rest unto your souls, For my yoke is easy, and my burden is light' (Matthew 11:29-30).

To the Galatian believers Paul could say, 'Stand fast therefore in the liberty wherewith Christ hath made us free' (Galatians 5:1). As to this word 'liberty', Mr Vine writes on *Eleutheria* (the Greek original):

> 'The phraseology is that of manumission from slavery which among the Greeks was effected by a legal fiction, according to which the manumitted slave was purchased by a god: as the slave could not provide the money the master paid it into the temple treasury in the presence of the slave, a document being drawn up containing the words 'for freedom'. No one could enslave him again, as he was the property of the god. Hence the word *apeleutheros*. In 2 Corinthians 3:17 the word denotes freedom of access to the presence of God. Here the fuller word brings out the spiritual emancipation in contrast to the natural freedman (*eleutheria*).'
> *Expository Dictionary of New Testament Words* p.461.

The force of all this is yet further emphasized in the picture of the Hebrew servant at the moment of his release (Exodus 21:3-6). The stated conditions were that if he was married when he was bought, then when he reached the seventh year of his bondage, his wife and family would be released with him; but if his master had given him a wife during that period, she would not be free to leave with her husband, but would remain the property of the slave master. The only way in which the family could then remain united was by the freed man rededicating himself to his master and voluntarily accepting a life time of bond service. Realising the certain loss of his wife and family under this law, and bearing in mind his agreeable conditions of service, he would say, 'I love my master, my wife, and my children; I will not go out free. Then his master shall bring him unto the judges; he shall also bring him to the door, or unto the door-post; and his master shall bore his ear through with an aul; and he shall serve him for ever' (Exodus 21:5-6).

The spiritual character of this dedication is enhanced when we note that the Hebrew word for 'judge' here and in other instances is *Elohim*. The judge stands in place of *Elohim*.

We would be doing less than justice to this subject if we failed to remark that our Lord in the days of His flesh, was the prime fulfilment of this interesting type, and, therefore, our service should be, within our limited powers, a copy of His own. The prophetic Scriptures make allusion to the pierced ear being fulfilled by the Saviour. As in humble obedience to His Father, He daily places Himself in the role of Jehovah's perfect bondservant. 'Sacrifice and offering, thou didst not desire, mine ears hast thou opened' (margin—digged) (Psalm 40:6), and again, 'The Lord God hath given me the tongue of the learned (lit. 'The well trained scholar'), that I should know how to speak a word in season to *him that is* weary' (lit. 'sustain the weary with a word'). He wakeneth morning by morning, he wakeneth mine ear to hear as the learned. The Lord hath *opened mine ear*, and I was not rebellious, neither turned away back (Isaiah 50:4-5). Such was His service in life, and in death, as He submitted Himself to the tortures of Calvary. 'I gave my back to the smiters, and my cheeks to them that plucked off the hair: I hid not my face from shame and spitting' (Isaiah 50:6). Jeremiah uses the phrase, 'I spake unto *rising up early*' (Jeremiah 7:13 and elsewhere): referring to which E.H. Plumptre says:

> 'A characteristic phrase by Jeremiah only signifying the highest form of human activity waking from sleep at the dawn of day to represent the like activity in God.'

All this leaves no room for surprise, that when Jehovah says 'Behold my servant' (Isaiah 52:13), it is referring to One who was obedient in death, with 'visage marred more than any man's' verse 14, then 'exalted and extolled and made very high' verse 13, and finally reigning in righteousness when He shall 'sprinkle many nations; the kings shall shut their mouths at Him' verse 15, or 'so will many nations marvel at Him.' (NIV footnote).

II

We would be too restrictive in our interpretation of service if we confined it to all activities immediately concerned with the christian ministry in its various branches, or the diversified levels of commitment on the part of its workers. It is therefore equally glorifying to God when a man pursues his secular calling in a manner that enhances the concept of service. Paul recognised the truth of this when he wrote, 'Let every man abide in the same calling wherein he was called. Art thou called *being* a (bond) servant? care not for it; but if thou mayest be made free, use it rather.' (1 Corinthians 7:20-21). In the circumstances of slavery in Paul's day, as we have already remarked, it mattered not provided the bond slave was Christ's freeman, or the freeman Christ's servant. The man's relationship to Christ was the important thing.

In similar manner he addresses himself to the bondservants in the Colossian church (Colossians 3:22-25), on the assumption that the servant will not seek to alter his status.

The servant was expected to submit in obedience to his master with integrity, not for fear of his master but 'fearing God' (v.22).

Moreover, he was to regard his secular employment not so much as a means of benefiting his master or himself, but was to labour 'as to the Lord' and not to men (v.23).

The man would know that, 'of the Lord ye shall receive the reward of the inheritance: for ye serve the Lord Christ' (v.24). This reward could be either in material benefits, or as an example of even greater faith, at the Judgment Seat of Christ. Similarly, unfaithful service could result in humiliation on both counts.

In all service there must be a worthy motive. Paul, again, stated it in the case of service to fellow believers, 'by love serve one another' (Galatians 5:13), and this of course is a principle which stems from a prior love for the Master.

When Peter was confronted by the risen Lord with his threefold denial of Him before the crucifixion, he was constrained to make a threefold confession of devotion, as the question was addressed to him, 'Lovest thou me?', with the exacting commission to what is probably the highest form of service in the church, 'Feed my sheep'. It was not to be his vocation because of its attraction for its own sake, nor because he would especially love the Lord's flock; but in loving the Saviour he would be fitted to better serve the saints, as he did both by word and letters (John 21:15-17).

A very important facet of this subject must be the quality of our service. At its highest it is offered in the first place to God before there is anything in it for man. Four of the New Testament writers use the word *Latreuo* which conveys this idea. It was said of Anna that she *'served God* with fastings and prayers night and day' (Luke 2:37) in the temple. The 'great multitude...before the throne, and before the Lamb...*serve* him day and night *in his temple'* (Revelation 7:9, 15). Again in the final state where there is no night 'the throne of God and of the Lamb shall be in it: and his servants shall *serve* him' (Revelation 22:3).

Dr Robert Young in his Concordance renders the word, 'to serve God' as 'public or rational service', whilst Dr Handley Moule translated it as 'worshipping service'. When Paul exhorted the Roman christians he said, 'Present your bodies a living sacrifice, holy, acceptable unto God, *which is* your reasonable service', i.e. 'rational service' (Romans 12:1).

One gathers from this that no service is of value except it is offered in the spirit of worship; God must have His first place in all things. Some have gone so far as to lay down that no service should be done before one celebrates the Lord's supper. This seems to be a misconception of what the Spirit indicates, i.e. that worship is of *first importance* relative to the service of, and for, God. Regard for obedience to the Lord would of course forbid our engaging in any form of service instead of partaking of the supper, but circumstances which do not contravene this principle would not seem to justify such a restrictive rule. To make unnecessary regulations which fail to have the support of Scripture amount to legalism and should be avoided. If one *prefers* to celebrate the supper first, *in time*, that is quite a different matter and does not deny another his liberty.

Finally, Leah's word 'hire' may be rendered 'reward', as we have already remarked, and where the servant of the Lord has used his Spirit-imparted gifts to the glory of God and for the edification of the church, or in the propagation of the gospel, the Lord's assessment of his service will be a welcome event.

In all humility we would say 'when ye shall have done all those things which are commanded you, say, We are unprofitable servants: we have done that which was our duty to do' (Luke 17:10).

Elders have a duty toward those whom they seek to guide in the church, the faithful among them 'watch for your souls, as *they that must give account*, that they may do it with joy, and not with grief' (Hebrews 13:17).

Not only to elders, but to all, the Scripture says, 'why dost thou judge thy brother? or why dost thou set at nought thy brother? for we shall all stand before the judgment seat of Christ' (Romans 14:10). In the light of this Paul writes, 'Judge nothing before the time, until the Lord come, who both will bring to light the hidden things of darkness, and will make manifest the counsels of the hearts: and then shall every man have praise of God' (1 Corinthians 4:5). One can only believe that in that day the Lord will reveal all that has been done for His glory, however obscure it may be, and be able to say 'Well done, *thou* good and faithful servant; thou hast been faithful over a few things, I will make thee ruler over many things: enter thou into the joy of thy lord' (Matthew 25:21).

This solemn event was directed to the Corinthian believers as a warning that rewards for service which the Lord evidently longs to confer might well be withheld since he introduced 1 Corinthians ch.3 with the words, 'I brethren, could not speak unto you as unto spiritual, but as unto carnal, even as unto babes in Christ' (v.1).

He reminds them that the believer is seen first as an *husbandman* whose sole preoccupation is to 'plant' and 'water' the good word of God to the 'babes in Christ'. Beyond this he cannot go for 'God gave the increase' (vs. 6, 7).

So the first test of profitable service is fruitfulness, something our Lord so much desired of His disciples who were encouraged to consider themselves as branches of the True Vine, saying, 'If ye abide in me, and my words abide in you, ye shall ask what ye will; and it shall be done unto you. Herein is my Father glorified that ye *bear much fruit*; so shall ye be my disciples' (John 15:7-8).

Secondly, Paul likens the believer to builders of the *house of God* which is built upon the sure foundation, 'for other foundation can no man lay than that is laid, which is Jesus Christ' (1 Corinthians 3:11). The materials are of varied quality, at best they are likened to 'gold, silver, and precious stones' by which, as Paul tells Titus, the servant may 'adorn the doctrine of God our Saviour in all things' (Titus 2:10). These materials representing all that glorifies God in our lives, will not only endure the refining fire of judgment but in the nature of such things will come forth purified and refined.

The servant may find the labour arduous, but God has promised that He 'will render to every man according to his deeds: To them who by patient continuance in well doing seek for glory and honour and immortality, eternal life...glory, honour, and peace, to every man that worketh good' (Romans 2:6, 7, 10).

Men heed thee, love thee, praise thee not
The Master praises—what are men?
(Bonar).

12

Zebulun (Dwelling)

'We, according to his promise look for new heavens and a new earth, wherein dwelleth righteousness' (2 Peter 3:13).

In view of the spiritual decline of the professing church seen in the example of Laodicea, any despondency the believer may suffer, as he is aware of its baneful influence, is compensated by a certain hope as he turns his thoughts to the imminent return of the Lord, promised in John's Gospel (John 14:2).

This prospect of being 'for ever with the Lord' enables us to say confidently with David, 'I will dwell in the house of the Lord forever' (Psalm 23:6). All this is suggested in the name of Leah's sixth and last true son, Zebulun (Dwelling).*

We gather from the prophetic word that our habitation in the eternal dwelling place, the new heaven, does not occur immediately after the rapture of the church at Christ's coming, though she will be 'with the Lord' and not be denied His promised 'comforts' (1 Thessalonians 4:18). It is therefore intended, on this account, to make no

*The biblical usage of the word 'Dwelling' embodies the idea of an extended period. Lot left his nomadic life with Abraham to *dwell* in Sodom. (Genesis 13:12) and Elimelech left Bethlehem in the time of famine to *dwell* in Moab (Ruth 1:1, 2 and 4). Insofar as the hope of the church is concerned, its duration is of course eternal.

more than a passing reference to intervening events since they are outside the scope of our subject, and deserve a comprehensive study in their own right.

Briefly then, we assume that since we are told that 'the time *is come* that judgment must begin at the house of God': (1 Peter 4:17) that the 'Bema' or Judgment Seat of Christ will be the occasion of the first judgment. A concensus of opinion, gathered from reliable commentators and translators, suggests that although it is true that the church of God has been judged for its works from its formation (Revelation 2 and 3 etc), it will be after the coming of Christ when the Christian's service will be under review by the Lord, and everything done for His glory suitably rewarded.

Following this impartial review there will then be the righteous judgments when men and nations face retribution as their deeds are inevitably brought to light.

Only then will the church of Christ assume the undeserved role of His Bride at the celebration of the Marriage Supper of the Lamb, when in all her glory and purity, redeemed and sanctified by the blood of Christ, she is united to Him (Revelation 17:7-9).

After this, the Lord, as the Son of Man, will put down all human government, which, having served its purpose, will give place to His reign on earth for a thousand years. During this millennium Satan will have been bound in chains and cast in the abyss, and sealed there by an avenging angel until its expiry, later to be released for 'a little season' at its termination (Revelation 20:1-3, 7-8). After his final defeat he will be judged and condemned to his eternal doom (v.10) together with his rebel hordes.

It is then that the church will people the new heaven, its eternal dwelling place, while the righteous ones of earth, who lived for God before and after the church's time-span during the Millennium, will eventually find their home in 'the new earth', which will give God in the ages to come, an earthly and an heavenly people, both chosen in Christ before the first creation.

II

Scriptures referring to conditions which will obtain for the glorified church are not numerous and are often expressed in symbolic language; the negative form is at times adopted when some unwelcome feature of earthly life is said to be absent (Revelation 21:4). This seemingly sparse amount of description of the new heaven is readily explained when one considers that the Spirit of God is imparting transcendent truth whilst using earthly language. It was said of Abraham's seed that they having 'died in faith, not having received the promises (of God), but having seen them afar off, were persuaded of *them* and embraced them, and confessed that they were strangers and pilgrims on the earth' (Hebrews 11:13). Our persuasion is of a similar order.

If we are to interpret the teaching of Scripture rightly we will deduce that the first essential condition applicable to the eternal state is that

God's will is to 'be done on earth *as it is in heaven*', where everything will be subjected to it. This is confirmed by some words of Paul on the same subject, 'Then *cometh* the end, when he (Christ) shall have delivered up the kingdom to God, even the Father; when he shall have put down all rule and all authority and power. For he must reign, till he hath put all enemies under his feet...And when all things shall be subdued unto him, then shall the Son also himself be subject unto him that put all things under him, that God may be all in all' (1 Corinthians 15:24-25, 28). The Saviour's ready submission at all times to his Father's will was seen, for example, when with his disciples he resorted for prayer, 'as he was wont, to the mount of Olives', immediately before His passion, and prayed, 'Father *if thou be willing*, remove this cup from me: nevertheless *not my will*, but thine be done' (Luke 22:39, 42).

A further feature of the new heaven will be that it is a place of eternal rest. This is suggested by the familiar verse from the Revelation 'Blessed are the dead which die in the Lord from henceforth; Yea, saith the Spirit, that they may rest from their labours; and their works do follow them' (Revelation 14:13). This statement is placed in contrast to the one describing those who worship Satan's human representative during the period of the Great Tribulation and who, as punishment, 'have no rest day or night, who worship the beast and his image (14:11). Although the promise is to the martyrs of that time, following the church's translation, it is equally true that all who have laboured and suffered for Christ's sake will find eternal peace in the new heaven.

The New Testament writer thinking of Joshua who led the Israelites into the Promised Land after their tedious wilderness wanderings, who without doubt, expected then to see the end of their trials, wrote, 'if Joshua had given them rest, God would not have spoken later about another day. There remains, then, a Sabbath rest for the people of God' (Hebrews 4:8 NIV). Those Hebrew Christians could rejoice in the fact that 'Now we who have believed enter that rest' (v.4). But for that nation at large, it still remains that some (i.e. those received into the church) will enter that rest. Those who formerly had the Gospel preached unto them, did not go in because of their disobedience (Hebrews 4:6). As members of the church, if such we are, we may find a large measure of support for the statement by Walter Scott:

> 'The term 'his rest' (Hebrews 3 and 4) in
> its fullest application refers to the eternal
> state'.

It is possible even in convulsive times that we may lose our sense of Christ's promised rest (Matthew 11:28). In such circumstances the Psalmist anticipates the problem as he exhorts us, '*Return unto thy rest,* O my soul' Psalm 116:7. A. Eidersheim says of this verse:

> 'The word "rest" is put in the plural, as
> indicating complete and entire rest at all
> times and in all circumstances'.

This rest is not to be a state of mere inactivity, but expresses an attitude of mind which is tranquil while bearing the yoke (Matthew 11:29) and in

repose as one walks before the Lord, in the land of
the living (Psalm 116:9). Life will be lived to the full
for 'His servants shall worship Him—pay divine
honours to Him, and do Him holy service' (Revelation
22:3; Zechariah 14:21, Amplified Version).

Apart from these somewhat overt references to
God's dwelling place, its main details are described
in Revelation 21:1-7, and possibly 22:5 where the
subject is introduced with the words: 'I saw a new
Heaven and a new Earth' (21:1). This must not be
confused with earlier descriptions of the Millennial
Kingdom, which, though detailed in the Old
Testament and the Gospels more fully than is the
case with the final state, falls far short of it, since
during the Millennium sin will have been relentlessly
repressed. The Lord's prayer will then be answered,
'Thy will be done in earth as *it is* in heaven'
(Matthew 6:10), for sin will not then be absent as it
will be in the 'new heaven and the new earth'. This
new Creation will not be a reconstruction of matter
from the ashes of the old, the result of God's
judgments by fire (Revelation 20:11 and 2 Peter
3:10).

All will be new, with a distinction being made
between the church, God's heavenly people, and
the citizens of the new earth, those who had
peopled the earth during the Millennium including
the sealed companies of Israel and Judah, named in
Revelation chs. 7 and 14, who, as the redeemed
from that nation cannot be the so-called favoured
ones from the Jehovah Witnesses cult, as they
falsely claim, in face of the plain statements of
Scripture. The patriarchs too will share in the

Millennial glories, for 'many shall come from the east and west, and shall sit down with Abraham, and Isaac, and Jacob, in the kingdom of heaven' (Matthew 8:11). Then Abraham's vision will become a reality, he who, 'looked for a city which hath foundations, whose builder and maker is God' (Hebrews 11:10).

A major difference between the new order and the old is that 'there was no more sea' (Revelation 21:1). In the first creation, the seas as they came into being were pronounced 'good' (Genesis 1:9-10). This lovely feature of the newly-formed world, in the end became the 'troubled sea' of the fallen creation. It was fitting that even in the days of Christ's flesh, His divine power over the elements provoked men to say, 'What manner of man is this, that even the winds and the sea obey Him!' (Matthew 8:27).

The self-subsisting One, who was before creation, active in it, and its undisputed ruler during His lifetime, will in that day have no need of the seas, with all their tragic memories.

Within the new heaven will be the glorified church, variously called the bride (Ephesians 5:30-32) and the holy city or new Jerusalem 'prepared as a Bride for her Husband' (Revelation 21:2). This will be the eternal *dwelling place* of all the redeemed from the nations during the church age, i.e. those who are said to keep 'the sayings of this book' (22:9).* In

*This 'Holy City' is distinct from that which Abraham awaited by faith (Hebrews 11:10, 12, 22). His was a location which he longed for in the Millennium, the other describes the Bride of Christ, His glorified church of the eternal ages. The city of the patriarch's

the perfect state it is clear that there will be free concourse between God's heavenly and His earthly people from the respective spheres, as the 'new Jerusalem comes down from God out of heaven, adorned as a bride for her husband'.

The seer hears a great voice out of heaven saying, 'Behold, the tabernacle of God is with men, and he shall dwell with them...and God Himself shall be with them and be their God' (21:3 RV). What bliss to realise that after the long Millennial years since the marriage supper she is still seen as the bride and wife of Christ! As Walter Scott so aptly observes:

> 'A thousand years of love, blessedness and companionship with her Husband and Lover are but brief. She is eternally united to Him who died for her and is now about to enter a yet deeper character of blessedness in the unchanging rest and joys of eternity. She is regarded as yet wearing her bridal robes. No soil or spot, nothing to mar their lustre and no change in her bridal affections'.
>
> *Exposition of the Revelation of Jesus Christ* p.420.

The latter half of Revelation 21:3 states that in that dwelling place 'God Himself shall be with them, *and be* their God'. This tells us that apart from God's tabernacle being with His glorified people, '*God Himself* will dwell among them'. At the Saviour's birth the name Emmanuel was given

---

vision is called the 'beloved city' (20:9) and described in some detail in Ezekiel 45:6 and 48:15-19. For an authoritative commentary on this subject the reader is recommended to consult Thomas Newberry's supplement to the *Newberry Bible* (pp. 107-111).

Him, which being interpreted is 'God with us' (Matthew 1:23). In its final and complete fulfilment, our Lord's parting words to the disciples will be realised, 'Behold I am with you all the days till the full end of the age' (Matthew 28:20, *Young's Concise Critical Comments*). It was in the wilderness tabernacle that God first made His presence known to man as an individual worshipper who was privileged to draw near to God in that curtained temple. Our thoughts naturally turn to the prologue of John's Gospel as the writer heralds the coming of the Son incarnate, from His Father's presence, 'the Word was made flesh, and dwelt (lit. tabernacled) among us (and we beheld his glory, the glory as of the only begotten of the Father), full of grace and truth' (John 1:14). In true tabernacle fashion He was:

'Humbled for a season to receive a Name,
From the lips of sinners, unto whom He came;
Faithfully He bore it, spotless to the last,
Brought it back victorious, when from death
He passed.'

In the constant exchanges between the two manifestations of the eternal state the figure of the tabernacle aptly describes these movements. The important differences between God's presence among the people of Israel, as they journeyed, and also the coming of the Saviour in flesh, is that both will be surpassed by the eternal presence of the Godhead whether in the new earth or the new Heaven. Finality in its perfection will have arrived! We may well sing:

'Without a cloud between,
Lord Jesus haste the day;

The morning bright without a cloud
To chase our tears away.'

Furthermore, 'He shall *wipe away every tear* from their eyes' (v.4). There will be no broken hearts needing consolation; no more tears, even of repentance, as welcome as they are on earth, especially when in flood they once washed the Saviour's feet. Not even tears of joy, as of some sudden relief, for the words of the Master will be fully realised, 'that my joy might remain in you, and *that* your joy might be full' (John 15:11).

Again, 'there shall be no more death' for the 'King of terrors and terror of kings' will have had its sting removed, even on earth.

Paul could say in triumph, 'For thy sake we are killed all the day long; we are accounted as sheep for the slaughter. Nay, in all these things we are more than conquerors through him that loved us. For I am persuaded, that *neither death,* nor life...nor any other creature, shall be able to separate us from the love of God, which is in Christ Jesus our Lord' (Romans 8:36-39). Today we are given grace to triumph over death, in that day we shall be removed from its presence for ever, for 'the last enemy *that* shall be destroyed is death' (1 Corinthians 15:26).

Added to this, 'neither shall there be any more pain, for the former things are passed away' (Revelation 21:4). The extent to which John's brother apostle, Paul, could share his vision is also expressed in Romans, as he writes, 'I reckon that the sufferings of this present time *are* not worthy *to be compared* with the glory that shall be revealed in us'! (8:18). Those pains we bring upon ourselves, and the ones inflicted by others, not to mention the afflictions which are common to all fallen humanity, inevitably leave their mark, and will be with us until, for the first time, we are transformed into the Saviour's likeness. Now the face expresses its weariness and pain; then it will be surpassing joy, 'the glory that shall be revealed in us'.

The verses 5 to 7 restate important truths, i.e. 'I make all things new'—'these words are true and faithful'—'It is done'—'He that overcometh shall inherit all things'; so in spite of all our praiseworthy endeavours to be victorious in the fight, another earlier quotation proves beyond doubt that Satan is overcome in the end by one means only by the believers, 'by the blood of the Lamb, and by the word of their testimony' (Revelation 12:11); a final reminder that our eternal security and blessings derive from the cross of Christ alone.

When we began this study of the sons of Jacob, the firstborn Reuben was so named meaning, 'See a son'. Our first view of the glorified church sees this relationship with God to be eternally ratified. 'I will be his God, and he shall be my son' (v.7). What a precious assurance with which to take leave of God's unfolding of His eternal love for His people.

This vision but briefly describes the new heaven, but nevertheless contains everything we need to know for the present time; sufficient to indicate that since it was God who first expressed His love in the coming of the Saviour we can say with the beloved disciple, 'we have known and believed the love that God hath to us. God is love; and he that dwelleth in love *dwelleth in God,* and God in him' (1

John 4:16).

Heaven, His dwelling place, is where the full revelation of God Himself will be seen, together with the Son, in whom it pleased the Father all fulness should dwell (Colossians 1:19).

13

Joseph — 'God hath Taken Away'

THE REJECTED RULER

'In his humiliation his judgment *was taken away*...His life *is taken* from the earth'
(Isaiah 53:6 LXX; Acts 8:33).

We recall that prior to the birth of Joseph, Rachel had borne no son of her own. Those born to her handmaid, Bilhah (with her own connivance), clearly failed to satisfy her natural desires; not surprisingly, therefore, when at last Joseph was born she exclaimed, '*God hath taken away* my reproach', and with the same breath made a prediction, '*The Lord shall add* to me another son' (Genesis 30:23-24).

Jacob by this time having become father to ten sons, this, the eleventh, was to precede Benjamin by about seventeen years. This prophecy by Rachel was evidently of the Lord, and seems to indicate that Joseph and Benjamin must be regarded as a pair, which in fact, is confirmed by their later interwoven lives.

From the outset we have associated Rachel with Israel as a type, and like Israel's relationship with the Lord, she was first in time to enjoy her husband's devotion, something which we believe survived over the years, in spite of the earlier

disappointments which involved both Rachel and
Jacob when they were denied their first nuptial joy.
Now that Joseph was born, he enjoyed a special
bond with his father, as did Benjamin when the
time arrived. This very human touch prepares our
minds to recognise in Joseph special reasons for his
fitness to rule, when we consider the special
emphasis our Lord placed upon the intimate
relationship He enjoyed with His Father, even in
the years of His humility. Apart from this it was
Joseph's inherent virtues which later fitted him for
the exalted position he was to occupy among his
brethren (Luke 22:29). In view of this, Joseph
should never be compared on equal terms with his
brethren, apart from the possible exception of
Judah, of whom Christ came, and who typifies the
power and authority of His reign. Since Joseph
speaks of One bringing peace and prosperity to His
people, it requires the two, in but a limited way, to
show forth the glories of Christ in the coming day
of His power.

II

The name Joseph is derived from a common
Hebrew word, which is capable of having two
meanings; the first which Rachel expressed was 'He
shall take away' and the second 'He shall add'. These
seemingly contradictory meanings are explained by
Dr R Payne-Smith (Ellicott's Commentary) by the
following extract:

> 'She, Rachel, trusts no longer to 'love
> apples', but looks to God for the great

blessing of children. He hearkens to her prayer (as 1 Samuel 1:19). In calling his name Joseph, there is again a play on two words, for it may be formed from the verb 'take away' (Genesis 30:23) and would then mean 'He takes away', or it may signify, 'He adds', which is the meaning made prominent by Rachel.'

Our purpose is to use the two meanings for different periods in Joseph's life, but 'He takes away' must precede 'He adds', as we shall see. It is of considerable interest to note that 'He shall add' is rendered 'He shall increase' by Thomas Newberry; Joseph's later prosperity was the ultimate reward of his life, though the pathway to it was fraught with temporary set-backs.

Soon after Joseph's birth, far reaching changes were to occur in the family circle. God had prospered Jacob in the community of Laban and jealousies had occurred among his sons, coupled with their accusation that the wealth he had acquired was at their expense; this in spite of Jacob's vehement protestations that the Lord had blessed him. It proved a timely guidance from the Lord, 'return unto the land of thy fathers, and to thy kindred, and I will be with thee' (Genesis 31:3).

Although the family made its first move soon after this, the relatively short journey to Canaan proved to be strangely erratic, since fourteen years were spent moving from place to place for shorter or longer periods, interspersed with well-known incidents. Even before Jacob eventually reached Canaan it needed a further prompting from the

Lord, as He said, 'Arise, go to Bethel, and dwell there: and make thee an altar unto God' (Genesis 35:1).

Arriving at Bethel, not surprisingly, Jacob enjoyed a period of spiritual blessing for about three years. First the 'strange gods' were put away; probably a legacy from Laban's Babylonian origins, 'and be clean' said Jacob, no doubt being aware of the defilement of idolatry, to which his own family had for long adhered (Genesis 31:29-35). In a similar mode he ordered them, 'change your garments'; so that all vestiges of pagan contamination were thoroughly expunged.

The three formative years of Joseph's life that followed the family's arrival at Bethel, the place of God's choice, must have made a firm impression on him for good, and established him the 'man of God' he became during the years ahead. If God had a ruler in view, Satan sought to forestall His purposes by setting up his own false line of rulers. Esau's oligarchy was the result, and within a few years he had promoted within his Edomic territory, kings and dukes, 'before there reigned any king over the children of Israel' (Genesis 36:31). The earlier alien families of Ishmael and Esau eventually became one by the marriage of Esau with Bashemath, Ishmael's daughter (Genesis 36:3), a union heading a people with an hostility to Israel, which remains unto this present day.

In spite of this, God's original promise to Abraham even now holds good. 'A father among nations have I made thee...kings shall come out of thee...with all the land of Canaan for an everlasting possession; and I will be their God' (Genesis 17:5-6,8).

III

The aptness of Rachel's first choice of names for Joseph, 'He shall take away' was seemingly delayed until he was seventeen years of age, and keeping his father's sheep with his four half brothers, the surrogate sons of Jacob, by Bilhah and Zilpah; 'and he brought unto his father their evil report' (Genesis 37:2).

It is clear that the wholesome atmosphere of Bethel, coupled with the years of God's chastening, produced in Jacob 'the peaceable fruits of righteousness' as of one who was 'exercised thereby' (Hebrews 12:11). Joseph too appears to have been amenable to its fruitful influence.

Conversely it is equally apparent that unchaste parents may well produce a like kind, and leave themselves no room for complaint if their offspring inherit their own wayward tendencies. Joseph valued what was seen to be right, even in his formative years, and had the courage to openly condemn his brothers' evil practices. But this coupled with other family reasons caused his older brothers to be antagonistic towards him. He was obviously his father's favoured son, as the gift of the 'richly ornamented robe' (v.3 NIV) betokened. This may well have been an indication in Jacob's opinion, that Joseph would one day be worthy of a ruler's honours (Esther 8:15). Then there were Joseph's dreams; firstly, that of the cornfield scene in which his brethren's sheaves made obeisance to his own; secondly of the heavenly bodies when the 'sun, moon and stars,' said Joseph, 'made obeisance to me' (Genesis 37:6-9). Even Jacob administered a mild rebuke to his seemingly precocious son but at the same time, 'observed the saying' (v.11).

A crisis within the family was therefore brooding and needed no more than an opportune moment before Joseph's brethren could give vent to their suppressed hatred.

It was all natural enough. The elder brethren were keeping their sheep at Shecham, and Jacob assigned Joseph to see, and confirm, that all was well with them.

He was redirected to Dothan by a local herdsman, and as he approached his brethren and their flocks a conspiracy was hatched. 'Behold, this dreamer cometh, Come now therefore, let us slay him...we shall see what becomes of his dreams' (Genesis 37:19-20).

Reuben pleaded for his life, determined in his mind to drop him into a dry pit and later to release him secretly. The appearance at that moment of Ishmaelite traders afforded a rare opportunity for them to acquire some easy gains. Joseph was accordingly sold for thirty pieces of silver and eventually found himself a slave in Egypt. When Reuben returned he rent his coat in despair when he found Joseph to be missing. The deception, that Joseph was devoured by a wild beast, was compounded by the tearing apart, and dipping the coat in goat's blood to convince their father of his death, who 'rent his clothes, and put sackcloth upon his loins, and mourned for his son many days' (37:34).

IV

The story is no more than a faint picture of Israel's treatment of its Messiah in later years.

Christ the 'beloved' of the Father, came as the obedient One to seek and save the lost sheep of the house of Israel. Like Joseph he was 'hated without a cause', and sold for 30 pieces of silver, but unlike Joseph, his death was not enacted, but factual. As Paul writes, 'For he hath made him to *be sin* (a sin offering) for us, who knew no sin; that we might be made the righteousness of God in him' (2 Corinthians 5:21).

The overruling wisdom and love of God is seen both in the type and the substance of this story. In later years as Joseph's brethren fall in repentance before him he reminds them, '*God did send* me before you to preserve life' (Genesis 45:5), and again, '*God sent me before* you to preserve you a posterity in the earth, and to save your lives by a great deliverance. So now it was *not you that sent me hither, but God*' (v.8).

The overruling of God is seen even more clearly in the cross of Christ, as the following scriptures state:

'Him, being delivered by the determinate council and foreknowledge of God, *ye have taken* and by wicked hands have crucified and slain' (Acts 2:23).
'*He was taken* from prison and from judgment...for the transgression of my people was he stricken' (Isaiah 53:8).

'His life *was taken* from the earth' (Acts 8:33).

Rachel could have had little understanding of those words which first escaped her lips at Joseph's birth. 'He shall take away'; it reminds us that 'it behoved Christ to suffer and to rise from the dead' (Luke 24:46).

14

Benjamin—'Son of Sorrow'—'Benoni'

'Then shall be great tribulation, such as was not since the beginning of the world to this time, no, nor ever shall be'   (Matthew 24:21).

'And Rachel travailed, and she had hard labour, the midwife said unto her, Fear not; thou shalt have this child also. And it came to pass, as her soul was in departing (for she died) that she called his name Benoni (son of my sorrow), but his father called him Benjamin (son of my right hand)' (Genesis 35:16-18).

Some sixteen years had passed since Joseph, the last son of Jacob, had been born to Rachel, and then when all hope of the prophecy that fell from her lips at that time—'The Lord shall add to me another son' (Genesis 30:24)—seemed to have eluded her, instead of the event being a source of joy to both parents, it proved to be one of sorrow to mother and father alike, since dying in childbirth she named him 'Benoni'—'son of my sorrow'. Her insight proved to be only too true, but with greater vision Jacob called him Benjamin—'son of my right hand'. Before either of these predictions could be fulfilled, Jacob suffered added grief by the loss of his seventeen year old Joseph, through the treachery of his brethren; the subject of our last chapter.

The death of Rachel after so long a period of waiting affords a graphic prophetic picture. Having, so far, regarded her as a fitting type of Israel (her death at about the time of Joseph's rejection and assumed death, depicts the truth of Israel's hiatus for the duration of the church dispensation, as a result of and following, the crucifixion of Christ, Joseph's antitype. Apart from the sorrow at the time of Benjamin's birth, a further and even greater grief was caused to the family years later in Egypt when Benjamin was held hostage. We are mindful of the time when He who requires the past (Ecclesiastes 3:15) will call Israel to account, just as it occurred when Joseph's guilty brethren faced the very one whom they wronged years earlier.

The verse we quoted at the head of this chapter, concerning great tribulation, proceeding from the lips of the Saviour, demands our attention, and will be seen to refer particularly to Israel, if the entire context of the passage is considered (vs.2-44). Its clear simple language marks it as probably the most important statement on the subject in hand, from any part of Scripture.

To rightly understand it we must note that future events were described to the Lord's disciples as if they would be there to witness their fulfilment. The reason for this becomes clear when we recognise that at that time He was speaking to faithful disciples who were not yet part of the future church, but could better be described in the words of the prophets as 'the remnant' of Israel, i.e. faithful men of God who were awaiting the coming of the Kingdom of Christ the Messiah, in the midst of an unbelieving sinful race.

The question asked was, 'what *shall be* the sign of

thy coming, and of the end of the world?' (lit. 'completion of the age', Newberry) (Matthew 24:3). The signs He gave were 'wars and rumours of wars' and 'nation shall rise against nation and kingdom against kingdom; and there shall be famines, and pestilences, and earthquakes, in divers places' (vs.6-7).

In addition He warned them, 'Take heed that no man deceive you. For many shall come in my name, saying, I am Christ and shall deceive many' (vs.4-5). Furthermore He cautioned them that though *all these things must come to pass, but the end is not yet'* (v.6), and that, as serious as the events were that He envisaged, they were to be but 'the beginning of sorrows' (v.8).

Some will urge that the calamities named are nothing unusual, since the earth has never been free of them, nor is it strange to hear of someone claiming to be the Christ, even as John could write, 'ye have heard that *antichrist* shall come, even now are there many antichrists' (1 John 2:18). To resolve the problem, the Lord told His disciples a parable which stated—'Now learn the parable of the fig tree; When his branch is yet tender, and putteth forth leaves, ye know that summer is nigh: So likewise ye, when ye shall see all these things, know that it is near, even at the doors. Verily I say unto you, This *generation* shall not pass, till all these things be fulfilled.' (Matthew 24:32-34). The word 'generation' as puzzled many, and provoked speculation as to whether it is the Jewish race, that was intended, or the duration of a lifetime. The same word was used of the Lord when He foretold the destruction of Jerusalem (Matthew 23:35-36) which in fact occurred within 40 years from that time. We conclude therefore that the full force of the prophecy would be seen within the lifetime of those members of the Jewish remnant who would be alive at the time our Lord indicated by His signs. His hearers would be familiar with the words of Isaiah who likened 'the vineyard of the Lord of Hosts' to 'the house of Israel', (Isaiah 5:1-7) and had already heard the parable which identified the fig tree with Israel. 'A certain *man* had a fig tree planted in a vineyard; and he came and sought fruit thereon, and found none. Then said he unto the dresser of the vineyard, 'Behold, *these three years* I come seeking fruit on this fig tree, and find none: *cut it down; why cumbereth it the ground*?' (Luke 13:6-7).

The application of this parable to the rejection of Israel at that time needs no explanation, but when our Lord speaks of the 'fig tree putting forth leaves' we are referred to the time when once more that ancient people would show signs of revival as a nation. It is the reality of Israel's national importance as a powerful force in the world today, which pinpoints the time of the Lord's prophecy, and informs us that it is this singular event which separates the perilous times in which we live, from all that might be compared with them from the past.

II

To form a balanced view of the nature of Divine judgment it is appropriate for us to examine briefly a few of the principles which govern this subject, that we may avoid holding false notions of the character of God.

Such a mental image was formed in the mind of the servant of the nobleman in our Lord's parable of the Pounds, who excused his negligent ways by saying, 'I feared thee, because thou art an austere man; thou takest up that thou layest not down, and reapest that thou didst not sow' (Luke 19:21).

Such examples of God's past judgments will convince us that these were not made in the heat of the moment, as vindictive acts, but were the assessment of a series of human activities seen in relation to the just claims of God (Colossians 3:6-7).

(1) Man is condemned for his deliberate disobedience to the revealed will of God, as expressed by Himself, or through his rejection of one or other of the Triune Godhead (John 3:19).

(2) God's judgments of man are not hasty; He is long-suffering and forebearing, acting only when all hope or intention of repentance for sin has vanished. Judgment is His last resort, 'his strange work' (Isaiah 28:21-22).

(3) He discriminates between those who desire to live righteously and those who practise un-righteousness. Where there is failure on the part of the people, He makes provision for their recovery, the result of their repentance and confession (1 John 1:8-9).

(4) When a nation, or part thereof, through persistent sin brings upon itself God's just and righteous judgments, any remnant therein which fears and serves Him, will be spared such

punitive judgments, though they may bear the common sufferings of the race meanwhile (2 Timothy 3:8-12).

(5) Since God's judgments are based upon His inflexible justice, they never extend beyond the severity required to serve their ends. Where His appeal is finally rejected there remains no time limit to his separation from God which man's refusal brings about. True repentance always averts God's need for retribution (Matthew 12:41).

(6) All judgment has been committed to the Son of God. He Himself knew its full severity when He became our substitute on the Cross. His sacrifice, alone and unique, enabled God to receive atonement for man's sin. Reconciliation between Himself and sinful man is made possible through faith in Christ. (Man is reconciled to God, not the reverse as a certain hymn implies). 'It *is* the blood *that* maketh an atonement for the soul' (Leviticus 17:11) and, 'by one offering, he hath perfected for ever them that are sanctified' (Hebrews 10:14; John 5:21-22).

III

The first recorded universal judgment occurred during the days of Noah, when man's sin provoked God to say, 'My spirit shall not always strive with man' (Genesis 6:3). In view of the warning implied in the words, Noah was instructed to build an ark for the salvation of his family; and during its construction he preached the righteousness of God to the guilty race; as Peter comments, 'the longsuffering of God *waited* in the days of Noah, while the ark was preparing' (1 Peter 3:20). Thus the witness was maintained; the call for repentance was ignored; and God was left with no alternative to the destruction of the rebel race, and to renew it with the remnant which survived: Noah's own family. God's retribution for evil seen in the Flood, together with the destruction of Sodom and Gomorrah, are quoted frequently in the later writings of the Old Testament and also in the New, and serve as a pattern for all later judgments. In particular the destruction of the cities of the Plain has lessons of its own.

Their environment had no appeal to Abraham, the historic man of faith; conversely his nephew Lot, the typical worldly minded believer, yet called 'just Lot' (2 Peter 2:7), found the location of the cities a desirable place to follow his pastoral calling. God's revelation to Abraham of the imminent judgment proved that though the decision was irreversible, it would never fall on believer and unbeliever alike. Abraham's model intercession for Lot's family, which at first asked for the cities to be spared if the unlikely number of fifty righteous souls could be found within their walls, was reduced step by step to ten. This proved too many, and with less than ten there was no recourse other than the threatened holocaust. Three only escaped, 'so as by fire' and Abraham's faith enabled him to remark, 'Shall not the Judge of all the earth do right?' (Genesis 18:25).

The wickedness of the men of Sodom, as they made every attempt to practise their morally degrading sins hard by the house of Lot, was repeated in like manner at Gibeah, incidentally, *a city of Benjamin!* during the latter years of the Judges (Judges 19-21) with striking similarities (cf. Genesis 19:1-8 and Judges 19:22-28). We regard this as a prophetic incident, as we note its salient features, which will find its fulfilment during the 'Great Tribulation', when Israel will bear the brunt of its severity.

The period of the Judges, like our own times, was characterised by permissiveness. We are therefore not surprised to learn that a Levite had taken to himself a concubine! (Judges 19:1-2).

At some stage in their association, she left him to return to her father's house. The Levite later went to the home and persuaded her to return, after some delaying tactics on the part of her father (vs.3-10). On the return journey they experienced some difficulty in finding a night's lodgings, and arrived at Gibeah, *a city of Benjamin,* where a wayfaring man saw their plight and offered them his modest home for the night.

It was then that a crowd of ruffians, 'sons of Belial', made evil demands for the Levite's favours. As an indication of the Levite's moral state, he allowed the old man to offer the gang his own daughter together with the concubine, and the latter was pushed out of his house to suffer a night of disgusting abuse (vs.22-28). When morning came the poor wretch was found dead on the doorstep with her hands outstretched as if pleading to her Levite master for some small act of mercy.

The Levite, seeking to justify himself, performed the gruesome feat of dividing her body into twelve parts and dispatching one part to each of the tribes of Israel, as if to involve all the nation (vs.29-30).

Benjamin was called upon to explain how such a scandal could have been perpetrated within its territory, and threatened retaliation meanwhile by some one tenth of the fighting force of Israel. Benjamin was obdurate and would not listen to the pleading of its fellow Israelites. From within its numbers it mustered an army of twenty six thousand swordsmen, which included seven hundred slingers, whom it alleged, could aim within an hairbreadth! With their overwhelming majority Israel's forces might have counted on an easy victory, and had even asked counsel of God as to who should lead the attack. Although the Lord indicated that Judah should spearhead the attack, to their surprise and humiliation Benjamin defeated Israel with twenty two thousand slain. The Lord commanded Israel to go up the next day; this resulted in a similar defeat, and with only slightly less casualties.

Before mounting a third attack, 'Israel...came unto the house of God, and wept, and sat before the Lord, and fasted that day until even, and offered burnt offerings and peace offerings before the Lord' (20:26). At last Israel had the moral armament to warrant victory, and the Lord said, 'Go up: for tomorrow I will deliver them into thine hand' (v.28). Blind obedience may seem to be all that God requires, but heart preparation is also vital in our spiritual warfare as it was in the bloody battle of Gibeah.

The ensuing battle brought about the defeat of Benjamin; so devastating that out of the entire tribe a *tiny remnant of six hundred* men was all that was left of the tribe and these fled to the wilderness and took refuge in the rock Rimmon. No women or children were spared (Numbers 20:47).

In the heat of the moment the tribes of Israel swore that 'not any of us give his daughters unto Benjamin to wife' (Numbers 21:1). Thus a tribe of Israel was threatened with extinction.

The massacre was to be no cause for rejoicing in Israel, when it was realised that the loss of Benjamin as a tribe would leave an irreplaceable breach in the nation's composition which had been recognised to be of Divine providence from the days of Jacob (Genesis 49). By common consent, the people mourned the impending loss of Benjamin, and prayed, 'O Lord God of Israel, why is this come to pass in Israel, that there should be to day one tribe lacking in Israel?' (Numbers 21:3). A day of compulsory mourning was called at Mizpeh, with burnt offerings, peace offerings and an awareness of the need for national repentance; a census was demanded to discover any part of the nation which had failed to appear, and the people of Jabesh-Gilead was found to have ignored the call. Twelve thousand soldiers massacred the people of Jabesh-Gilead apart from four hundred virgins. These were then offered to the men of Benjamin as wives, and the two hundred Benjamites, without wives, were provided with wives from virgins who attended a feast of the Lord at Shiloh, from whence they were taken by the remaining two hundred single men.

'And the children of Benjamin did so, and took *them* wives, according to their number, of them that danced, whom they caught; and they went and returned unto their inheritance, and repaired the cities, and dwelt in them' (Judges 21:23). From such a decimated remnant the tribe of Benjamin was once more re-populated, though for centuries was still 'the smallest of the tribes of Israel' (1 Samuel 9:21).

The tragedy of Gibeah became a byword among the people of Israel, even six hundred years. later, when Hosea the prophet likened it to God's future judgment of Israel as a whole, rather than of one tribe, as a result of the nation's sin.

> 'They have deeply corrupted *themselves*, as in the days of Gibeah: *therefore* he will remember their iniquity, he will visit their sins' (Hosea 9:9).

To be yet more explicit, he used language which will apply only to the time of the Great Tribulation, when Israel will pass through 'the time of Jacob's trouble' (Jeremiah 30:7). This period will be incomparable for its severity, with any judgment at any time in history (Matthew 24:21).

We quote Hosea's words from the Amplified Version for greater clarity,

> 'The high places also of Aven (once Bethel, house of God, now *Beth-aven*, house of idols) the sin of Israel shall be destroyed, the thorn and the thistle shall

come up on their idol altars, and they shall say to the mountains, Cover us; and to the hills, Fall on us' (Hosea 10:8).

It will be recalled that when the Lord was being taken to Calvary, amidst the throng of sorrowing women, He turned to them quoting the self same words from Hosea.

'Daughters of Jerusalem, weep not for me, but weep for yourselves, and for your children. For, behold, the days are coming, in the which they shall say, Blessed are the barren, and the wombs that never bare, and the paps which never gave suck. Then shall they begin to say to the mountains, Fall on us, and to the hills, Cover us (Luke 21:28-30).

This fulfilment of Hosea's prophecy occurs in the book of the Revelation:

'And the kings of the earth, and the great men, and the rich men, and the chief captains, and the mighty men, and every bondman, and every free man, hid themselves in the dens and in the rocks of the mountains; And said to the mountains and rocks, Fall on us, and hide us from the face of him that sitteth on the throne, and from the wrath of the Lamb. For the great day of his wrath is come; and who shall be able to stand?' (Revelation 6:15-17).

Hosea continues his prophecy 'O Israel, you have *wilfully* sinned from the days of Gibeah (when you all but wiped out the tribe of Benjamin). There *Israel* stood *then, only* that the battle against the sons of unrighteousness might not overtake *and* turn against them at Gibeah (but now the kingdom of the ten tribes and the name of Ephraim shall be utterly blotted out) (Hosea 10:9, Amplified Version).

Judgment at this coming time will be tempered with mercy, for the Lord will declare, 'it is time to seek the Lord, to enquire *for*, and of Him *and* to require His favor, till He comes and teaches you righteousness *and* rains His righteous gift of salvation upon you' (v.12, Amplified Version).

'So all Israel shall be saved: as it is written, There shall come out of Sion the Deliverer, and shall turn away ungodliness from Jacob' (Romans 11:26).

It would seem that events from the time of the First World War have shed much light on prophetic fulfilment, which was not available to nineteenth century writers. It was not always clear to them that there would be a nation of Israel before the Lord's coming. The result of this has been that Jews from the free nations have returned in vast numbers to the 'land of promise'. In the nature of the case the immigrants must have included members of every tribe in addition to Benjamin and Judah, none of whom will then have claimed an inheritance to their final allotted territories (Appendix B).

The question then arises, What of the Israelitish people numbering some millions, who are prevented from leaving the countries behind the Iron Curtain? Their constant cry to migrate to the land of their possessions goes unheeded, apart that of a minority released from time to time as a result of strenuous diplomatic efforts on the part of the Western nations.

Soon, we believe, their longings will be realised with the coming of Christ, as the Son of Man. As our Lord Himself said,

> 'he shall send his angels with a great sound of a trumpet, and they shall gather his elect from the four winds, from one end of heaven to the other' (Matthew 24:31).

Isaiah's prophecy too will then be realised:

> 'I will bring my seed from the east, and gather thee from the west; I will say to the north, Give up; and to the south, Keep not back: bring my sons from far, and my daughters from the ends of the earth (Isaiah 43:5-6).

In this way will blessings come to the entire house of Israel following the sorrows of the Great Tribulation.

During those years that Benjamin grew into manhood, Joseph saw changes in his status from being a servant to Potiphar, the captain of the guard, to that of second in command in Egypt, under Pharaoh, as a reward for his integrity against formidable odds. As he freely acknowledged at the time of his reunion and reconciliation with his brethren, 'God sent me before you to preserve you a posterity in the earth' (Genesis 45:7).

It was all a question of the guilt of many years tormenting the consciences of Joseph's brethren until the moment came for the entire truth to be acknowledged, with heartfelt confession. After a testing time which must have amounted to despair, Joseph brought home to them the guilt of past years. That the experience was one of intense remorse we are left in no doubt. Apart from that, Joseph, with consummate skill, satisfied himself that their repentance was no superficial expediency, when he was informed that Benjamin, his own brother, by Rachel, occupied the same degree of affection which he, himself, had enjoyed during his own boyhood. The device of causing his divining cup to be put into Benjamin's sack would have given his brethren a ready-made excuse to denounce him had they so desired. His obvious yearning after his younger brother must not have passed unobserved, and the more than sufficient mess set before Benjamin in the presence of them all proved to be a test which none of them could have survived without revealing some lingering envy, had it been there.

We must weigh against the guilt of the brethren, grievous as it was to themselves and Joseph too, the undoubted love he felt toward them throughout the entire episode. This is seen clearly by the secret tears he shed, apart from the unconcealed ones, in spite of his brusque treatment of them. How often God has to deal with His people in this manner.

    'Judge not the Lord by feeble sense
    But trust Him for His grace
    Behind a frowning countenance
    He hides a smiling face.'

So it is with Israel, and so it will be when the time

comes for the nation once more to be restored to favour after the purifying judgments of God. He declares, 'the day cometh, that shall burn as an oven...the day that cometh shall burn them up, saith the Lord of hosts, that it shall leave them neither root nor branch. *But unto you that fear my name shall the Sun of righteousness arise with healing in His wings'* (Malachi 4:1-2).

V

The 'hour of trial', the 'Great Tribulation', 'the time of Jacob's trouble', as the period of Israel's judgments is variously called, will follow the home-call of the church: when 'the fulness of the Gentiles' is come. Then God will once more turn His attention to Israel, since the full complement of Gentile believers will have been incorporated in the church with a minority of people of Hebrew origin. Ere the 'joy of the morning' can dawn for Israel, the 'sorrow must endure for a night'!

Reference to the chart in the Appendix 'A' will indicate that following the church's translation, there will be a world-ruler energised by Satanic powers who will find it expedient to make a covenant with Israel for a seven year period. In the midst of this period he will renounce the covenant, and instead of being the pretended friend of Israel, will prove to be its most savage enemy of all time. His co-ruler, the Anti-Christ, will demand worship in the rebuilt Temple at Jerusalem and such will be the oppression that a minority only will survive the onslaught. 'It shall come to pass, *that* in all the land,

saith the Lord, two parts therein shall be cut off *and*
die; but the third shall be left therein. And I will
bring the third part through the fire, and will refine
them as silver is refined, and I will try them as gold
is tried: they shall call on my name, and I will hear
them: I will say, It is my people: and they shall say,
The Lord is my God' (Zechariah 13:8-9).

We believe that scripture and history both
indicate that Benjamin and Judah will bear the
brunt of these judgments at the hands of historic
hostile Northern nations, which will themselves be
destroyed by the 'appearing of Christ', in power as
Son of Man, as the prophet writes:

> 'Jerusalem shall be inhabited again in her
> own place, even in Jerusalem. The Lord
> also shall *save the tents of Judah* first...In that
> day shall the Lord defend the inhabitants
> of Jerusalem...And it shall come to pass in
> that day, *that* I will seek to destroy all the
> nations that come against Jerusalem.
> And I will pour upon the house of David...
> the spirit of grace and of supplications:
> and they shall look upon me whom they
> have pierced, and they shall mourn for
> him, as one mourneth for his only son'
> (Zechariah 12:6-10).

The decimation of Israel, or perhaps more
correctly at that time, Benjamin and Judah, will be
the fulfilment of the Gibeah type. In the years that
followed that awful massacre, Benjamin gradually
recovered its numbers once more. After another
one hundred and fifty years when a census was
taken, 'out of the tribe of Benjamin, that bare

shields and drew bows, were two hundred and fourscore thousand: all these *were* mighty men of valour' (2 Chronicles 14:8).

The increase among the people of Israel will be of comparable proportions. Up to the time of the Lord's appearing the two houses of Israel, Judah and Israel, divided from the time of Solomon's death, will remain apart, with Judah and Benjamin being mainly represented by the Jews in the land of Israel today; and in spite of every effort by the Northern powers to retain Israel in bondage in their lands, eventually they will have to yield to the overwhelming call of God for their return to their land, to share the glories of the Kingdom under their Messiah.

As Ezekiel wrote:

'Behold, I will take the children of Israel from among the heathen, whither they be gone, and will *gather them* on every side, and bring them into their own land. And I will *make them one nation* in the land upon the mountains of Israel; and *one king* shall be king to them all: and they shall be no more two nations, neither shall they be divided into two kingdoms any more at all' (37:21-22).

Paul, writing to the Roman believers makes a similar prophecy, saying:

'And so all Israel shall be saved: as it is written, There shall come out of Sion the Deliverer, and shall turn away ungodliness from Jacob: for this *is* my covenant unto them when I shall take away their sins...as touching the election, *they are* beloved for the fathers' sakes. For the gifts and calling of God *are* without repentance' (Romans 11:26-29).

It could be said of Israel, that which Paul wrote to the church at Corinth:

'I rejoice, not that ye were made sorry, but that ye sorrowed to repentance: for ye were made sorry after a godly manner... For godly sorrow worketh repentance to salvation not to be repented of: but the sorrow of the world worketh death' (2 Corinthians 7:9-10).

15

Joseph

'He shall add' (Genesis 30:24).
'He must increase' (John 3:30).

How little did Joseph's brethren realise that the
famine which drove them to Egypt for food for
themselves, and provender for their livestock,
would open the door to unimaginable blessings in
the land of their adoption, under the benign rule of
their absent brother. His earlier dreams had proved
to be nothing less than a fore-shadowing of God's
plan for the blessing of Israel's family through one
exalted to high office from among themselves.

The chastening effects of famine are often cited
in scripture where it was necessary to bring the
people of God to a realisation of their departure
from His ways. It was to reconcile them afresh to
Himself, and even to bring greater blessings than
those which they had known before; this occurred
with the family of Jacob, and, if we read the signs of
the times aright, it will soon be true of Israel to be
once more restored to favour with God and ushered
into the kingdom of their one-time rejected Saviour
and Messiah (Psalm 105:18-21).

We recognise in this type the future rule of the
One of whom the prophet Daniel wrote:

'There was given unto him dominion, and
glory, and a kingdom, that all people, and

languages, should serve him...his dominion
is an everlasting dominion, which shall
not pass away, and his kingdom *that* shall
not be destroyed' (7:14).

The exaltation of Joseph points to One greater
than himself, as Christ shall presently assume His
rightful place as 'King of kings', in a day we believe
to be near at hand. The imminence of that kingdom,
in the words of the Lord to His disciples, would be
signalled by events He described as 'the beginnings
of sorrows', which, apart from famines, presently
the scourge of vast areas of the earth's surface,
includes 'pestilences, earthquakes, international
turmoils including wars and rumours of wars'
(Matthew 24:4-8).

But an even greater famine is to be seen
wherever pagan religion or atheistic dominance
takes over any country and people. The prophet
Amos saw both the *literal and spiritual* famine which
would precede the Coming (appearance) of the Lord
to establish the Kingdom (Amos 8:11-12).

Commenting on this chapter, Reynolds and
Whitehouse (*Ellicott's Commentary*) remark:

'It is harvest time, the end of the
agricultural year. Israel is ripe for his final
doom, that will sweep down like a scythe
(v.2)...The words describe the reign of
death and doom—with none to bury or
make lamentation—a full end (v.3). Their
(merchants) money-making prosperity
was carried to such unscrupulous lengths,
that they even sold the refuse of corn,
little better than mere chaff (v.6). Such

will be the degree of famine in the last days.'

But so complete will be the hunger for God's word, that the prophet continues, 'I will send a famine in the land, not a famine of bread, nor a thirst for water, but of hearing the words of the Lord: And they shall wander from sea to sea, and from the north even to the east, they shall run to and fro to seek the word of the Lord, and shall not find it' (vs.11-12).

As we consider the situation in the Genesis story, the brethren, when they saw Joseph as the all-powerful ruler, they were themselves suffering the direst straits of famine. What a contrast it is. Joseph in full possession of the power and glory foreseen in his dreams, and his brethren having, at last, to acknowledge their utter dependence on him!

The extent of his glory is seen from the moment Pharaoh appointed him as he removed his ring from his hand and put it upon Joseph's hand' (Genesis 41:41-42). This was the signet ring which empowered Joseph to enact laws in the king's name. Then he was 'arrayed in vestures of fine linen' (v.42).

> 'In the east it is usual on all occasions of showing the royal favour to give changes of raiment, but there is here the further signification that as this 'fine white linen' was the special dress of the king and the priests, the bestowal of it indicated Joseph's admission to the ruling classes of Egypt' (R. Payne Smith).

Then

> 'He put a gold chain about his neck' seen

in the monuments as one of royal insignia 'and made him to ride in the second chariot that he had.' The object of this procession was to display Joseph to the people as their new governor. The Pharaoh probably took the chief part in this parade, riding in the first chariot of state.' (Ibid)

The following cry of the people, 'Bow the knee' (v.43) appears to be a mistranslation of the Hebrew, *abrech*, if, as Canon Cook explains, it means 'rejoice, be happy', it seems to the present writer a more likely response in that situation.

So complete was Joseph's authority, that Pharaoh said to Joseph, 'I am Pharaoh and without thee shall no man lift up his hand or foot in the land of Egypt' (v.44).

As if to confer a special Egyptian title upon Joseph, 'Pharaoh called Joseph's name Zaphnath-Paaneah' (v.45). Various meanings of this name have been given by different translators, most of which show general agreement.

"Saviour of the world" (Jerome, Newberry LXX).

"Food of life, or of the living" (Canon Cook).

Last, but not least, 'he (Pharaoh) gave him to wife, Asenath, the daughter of Potiphera, priest of On' (v.45). For Joseph to be able to present a Gentile bride, as he faced his once estranged brethren, completes a beautiful picture which generations of believers have recognised as a fitting symbol of the relationship which exists between Christ and His bride, the church.

The full measure of Joseph's brethren's confession of their past guilt, and of their ready acknowledgement of his present and future glory, was finally seen when Joseph first presented his sons to Jacob as he was nearing his life's end, with a view to the dying patriarch pronouncing his blessing upon them.

The sons of the family had even then misgivings about Joseph's intentions despite the reconciliation which had been made between them and himself. He sought to reassure them by saying, 'Ye thought evil against me; *but* God meant it unto good...to save much people alive...fear ye not: I will nourish you, and your little ones' (Genesis 50:20-21). These, Joseph's last recorded words, would become more meaningful as he named his two sons at the time he presented them to his father Jacob. His brethren would henceforth have no occasion for remorse.

The firstborn was named Manasseh (forgetting) 'For God, *said he*, hath made me *forget* all my toil, and all my father's house'...'The name of the second called he Ephraim' (fruitful): 'For God hath caused me to be fruitful in the land of my affliction' (41:51-52). These two sons were later given the honour to become the founders of two tribes which bear their names. Levi, originally one of the twelve entitled to an inheritance in Canaan, forfeited that right when it was chosen as the priestly tribe of Israel, and one of Joseph's sons replaced it. Joseph too, for a very different reason, as the typical ruler, could not share a portion *with* his brethren, since he was to be *above* them by far in rank. His two sons would be

assigned their narrow strips of territory in the
Millennial Kingdom with all the blessings pertaining,
but Joseph's blessing from Jacob was of quite a
different order:

> 'The blessings of thy fathers have prevailed
> above the blessings of my progenitors,
> unto the utmost bounds of the everlasting
> hills: they shall be on the head of Joseph,
> and on the crown of the head that was
> separate from his brethren' (Genesis
> 49:26).

In time Ephraim came to be regarded as the
representative name for the ten tribes in the
division of the Kingdom after Solomon's reign, and
Judah and Benjamin were to enjoy a special
relationship as will be seen later. Joseph was a true
type of the Lord who promised His disciples, 'I
appoint unto you a kingdom, as my Father has
appointed unto me' (Luke 22:29).

II

Christ the antitype, ruling and reigning:

> 'There were great voices in heaven saying, The
> kingdoms of this world are become *the king-
> doms* of our Lord and of his Christ: and he
> shall reign for ever and ever' (Revelation
> 11:15).

Turning to the antitype we bring together a brief
selection of prophetic passages of Scripture relating
to Christ the King of Israel, and intimating the
character of His Kingdom. Their available number
is legion and would have been more readily

understood by generations of Bible readers if theologians of the past had not confused the blessings of the church, with the rightful claims of Israel. The Psalms and Prophets abound with details of Christ's earthly Kingdom if the Scriptures are approached with an open mind under the Spirit's guidance.

In using the term 'the last days' we are borrowing a term widely used in the Old Testament Scriptures, and on a few occasions in the New Testament. This refers to events leading up to, and including, the coming (*parousia*) of the Lord, the 'great tribulation', the Marriage of the Lamb (Revelation 19:7), and the 'appearing' of Christ as Son of Man to bear judgment, and as King of kings to reign in the millennial age, prior to the last judgment and the eternal age. The lengthy church era during which grace has reigned, has caused many to say, 'Where is the promise of his coming? for since the fathers fell asleep; all things continue as *they were* from the beginning of the creation' (2 Peter 3:4). That God is about to intervene in man's affairs in miraculous ways is beyond their comprehension!

Taking the example of past ages will indicate that miracles were seen at specified times when God was introducing some new feature relating to man's destiny. They were shortlived, with long periods between each. The creation and the time of the Exodus are the earliest examples, followed by the time of the prophets of Israel, and the later incarnation of the Saviour, and the founding of the church on the day of Pentecost (Acts 2:1, 33, 47).

It is by 'signs' or miracles that man is convinced

that God is furthering His purposes. The second coming of Christ will be the first such event heralding the imminent millennial Kingdom, which, as we have already noted, will be peopled by the remnant of redeemed Israel that will accept Christ as King and Redeemer at His appearing.

A remnant from the nation of Israel, having been sorely visited by Divine judgment for its sins, with many from Judah and Benjamin enduring the first severe visitation, will finally be represented by the entire nation when the Lord's words will be literally fulfilled, 'then shall appear the sign of the Son of man in heaven; and then shall all the tribes of the earth mourn, and they shall see the Son of man coming in the clouds of heaven with power and great glory. And he shall send his angels with a great sound of a trumpet, and they shall gather together his elect (from all the tribes), from the four winds, from one end of heaven to the other' (Matthew 24:30-31).

It will be the moment when Christ will deliver His people in their hour of deepest need.

The Northern powers under the symbol of Gog and Magog will consider this an opportune time to utterly destroy all trace of the nation of Israel and, in so doing, will think to frustrate God's eternal purposes. The Lord will have the last word, saying:

'I...will cause thee to come up from the north parts, and will then bring thee upon the mountains of Israel: And I will smite thy bow out of thy left hand, and will cause thine arrows to fall out of thy right hand. Thou shalt fall upon the mountains of Israel, thou, and all

thy bands, and the people that *is* with
thee...Behold, it is come, and it is done saith the
Lord God; this is the day whereof I have
spoken. And they that dwell in the cities of
Israel shall go forth, and shall set on fire and
burn the weapons...with fire seven years...and
they shall spoil those that spoiled them...saith
the Lord God. I will give unto Gog a place there
of graves in Israel...and there they shall bury
Gog, and all his multitude: and they shall call it
the valley of Hamon-gog. And seven months
shall the house of Israel be burying of them,
that they may cleanse the land' (Ezekiel 39:2-4,
8-12).

So did the prophet describe Christ's coming
victory at Armageddon.

After these far-reaching judgments, Israel will
enjoy a *Millennium of peace,* her 'Sabbath of rest',
unlike anything known hitherto.

'The wolf also shall dwell with the lamb,
and the leopard shall lie down with the
kid; and the calf and the young lion and
the fatling together; and a little child shall
lead them...the earth shall be filled with
the knowledge of the Lord, as the waters
cover the sea' (Isaiah 11:6, 9).

In that day, 'the Lord shall be king over all the
earth...there shall be one Lord and his name one'
(Zechariah 14:9).

'A kingdom, which shall never be destroyed'
(Daniel 2:44).

'Behold, a king shall reign in righteousness, and
princes shall rule in judgment' (Isaiah 32:1).

Famine will be banished: 'the seed *shall be* prosperous, the vine shall give her fruit, and the ground shall give her increase, and the heavens shall give their dew; and I will cause the remnant of this people to possess all these *things*' (Zechariah 8:12).

The curse will be lifted and all nature delivered of its scourge.

'The wilderness and solitary place shall be glad for them; and the desert shall rejoice, and blossom as the rose...The lame *man* shall leap as an hart; and the tongue of the dumb sing...for in the wilderness shall water break out and streams in the desert (Isaiah 35:1,6).

Mankind will have *a desire to know the Lord* for 'many nations shall come, and say, Come, and let us go up to the mountain of the Lord, and to the house of the God of Jacob; and he will teach us his ways, and we will walk in his paths' (Micah 4:2).

Longevity will be enjoyed by its citizens when at last Jerusalem their capital shall be a place of true joy.

'There shall be no more thence an infant of days, nor an old man that hath not filled his days: for the child shall be an hundred years old, but the sinner *being* an hundred years old shall be accursed...as the days of a tree *are* the days of my people, and mine elect shall long enjoy the work of their hands. They shall not labour in vain' (Isaiah 65:20, 22-23).

'Jerusalem shall be called a city of truth; and the mountain of the Lord of hosts the *holy mountain.* Thus saith the Lord of hosts; There shall yet old men and old women dwell in the streets of Jerusalem, and every man with his staff in his hand for very age. And the streets of the city shall be full of boys and girls playing in the streets thereof. Thus saith the Lord of hosts' (Zechariah 8:3-6).

The foregoing verses are but a small selection of the hundreds of Messianic prophecies speaking of the Lord, the King, and His Kingdom. Both Israel and the church will be involved in different ways, sharing the responsibilities of the administration of the kingdom.

These Old Testament prophecies were the basis of the Messianic hope throughout the ages of the prophets; but Paul could equally anticipate this long-awaited time of peace. He wrote, 'the whole creation groaneth and travaileth in pain together until now. And not only *they,* but ourselves also, which have the firstfruits of the Spirit, even we ourselves groan within ourselves, waiting for the adoption, *to wit,* the redemption of our body' (Romans 8:22-23).

Christ is not merely the hope of the church, He is equally the hope of all mankind, and of Israel (Jeremiah 14:8).

16

Benjamin — Son of My Right Hand

SHARING THE GLORY

The full scale prophetic picture of Israel in the Millennium was given by Moses as he was about to depart (Deuteronomy 33). The review is vastly different from that of Jacob's (Genesis 49). In the later passage Israel is in full possession of millennial blessings, and in favour with God. No word of censure is spoken; no tribe fails to be blessed;

'of Benjamin he said, The beloved of the Lord shall dwell in safety by him; *and the Lord* shall cover him all the day long, and he shall dwell between His shoulders' (Deuteronomy 33:12).

The literal translation from the Hebrew suggested from Ellicott's commentary reads as follows:

'Unto Benjamin he said, Beloved of Jehovah. He (Jehovah) will dwell in security upon him, covering him over all the day, and between his shoulders (mountain slopes) He hath taken up His abode.' It is generally agreed that this blessing points to the site of the place out of all the tribes of Israel, Jerusalem in the tribe of Benjamin' (C H Waller MA).

In the details taken from 'The Scroll of Time' by John Ashton Savage (Appendix B) it will be seen from the chart that when Ezekiel's temple is to be built (chs.47,48) the considerable sized apportionment of territory devoted to it will be flanked by Judah to the north, and Benjamin to the south, and Benjamin will have conveyed it from its own entitlement from ancient times. (See Judges 1:21.) It would appear that the two tribes will enjoy a privileged nearness to the Lord's temple during the Millennium, a matter of great importance at such a time.

We have in the story of Asa, king of Judah (BC 941), a situation which is strikingly similar to that in which Judah and Benjamin will find themselves in some future day (2 Chronicles 14 to 16), and in the end with the same kind of promised blessings.

We read, 'Now for a long season Israel hath been without the true God, and without teaching priest, and without law. But when they in their trouble did turn unto the Lord God of Israel, and sought him, he was found of them' (2 Chronicles 15:3-4).

Asa had come to the throne during a critical period of the nation's history. Idolatry was rife, he removed 'high places' 'images and groves' all associated with strange pagan gods. He even removed his mother from being queen because of her idolatry (2 Chronicles 15:16).

As a positive step, 'he commanded Judah to seek the Lord God of their fathers, and to do the law and the commandments' (2 Chronicles 14:4).

During this period of revival Zerah the Ethiopian brought an army, a million strong, against Judah and Benjamin. (Of the many references to Ethiopia in Scripture do we not find one that shows a friendly disposition toward Israel!)

As a result of the impending threat Asa prayed, 'Lord it is nothing with thee to help, whether with many, or with them that have no power: help us O Lord our God; for we rest on Thee, and in Thy name we go against this multitude. O Lord, thou art our God; let not man prevail against thee (14:11). So the Lord smote the Ethiopian before Asa, and before Judah and the Ethiopian fled' (v.12).

Following the victory, the prophet Azariah was sent of God to Asa with the following far-seeing promise:

> 'Hear ye me Asa, and all Judah and Benjamin; the Lord is with you while ye be with Him. And if ye seek Him, he will be found of you. But if ye forsake Him, he will forsake you' (15:2).

Although like many other typical characters Asa, to his great cost, failed during the last three years of his reign, even after thirty six years of the enjoyment of God's blessing, nevertheless Hanani the prophet reminded him, 'Were not the Ethiopians and Lubims a huge host with very many chariots and horsemen. Yet because thou didst rely on the Lord He delivered them into thine hand. For the eyes of the Lord run to and fro throughout the whole earth to shew himself strong in the behalf of them whose heart is perfect toward Him' (16:8-9).

In a similar manner the ordering of the Kingdom will demonstrate the power and glory of Christ, and His ability to suppress all evil. Suppression however is not regeneration, and in spite of the stringent controls exercised during the Millennium age it will be seen that man, given his final chance to obey and serve God in freedom will yet prove to be rebellious. Satan is to be released from his chains 'for a little season', only to be sent to his eternal doom with his faithless dupes. Man's final opportunity to submit to God's will having been thrown away after seeing His glorious rule, robs man, at the last, of any excuse for his rejection.

The final solution is seen only when the new heaven and the new earth is created and the church inherits the former, with Israel occupying the latter, eternally. The issues are far too serious to be ignored, 'so much the more as we see the day approaching.'

17

Conclusion

As we have considered God's dealings with man from the days of faithful Abraham unto the end of time, as to both Israel and the church, our readers may well ask, 'in view of the prevailing confusion, men and brethren, what shall we do?'

We have sought to show from the Word, the course of both apostate Christianity and its tragic end, and also the works of God which can never fail. But what of the present?

It would be unacceptable to cut the ground from under the feet of those who find themselves in the company of apostate Christendom, with its false objectives, without suggesting an alternative course of action. Fortunately there is another way, apart from that advocated by those seeking to form a vast federation of churches from every persuasion and even faiths which utterly refuse to acknowledge the Deity of Christ, and which threaten to swallow up all forms of professed Christian testimony. This will, we believe, take place when once all true believers are removed from the scene at the coming of the Lord.

On their part, it is no longer considered necessary to accept the Scriptures as the final arbiter for faith and practice. Indeed the most vocal critics are those found within the broad fold of Christendom.

The only alternative is demonstrably to return to

the Scriptures for guidance. But some will say, 'Doesn't the church teach? Have we not to listen to its voice?' The answer to such questions must be an emphatic 'No'. Scripture must be the basis for teaching. The church needs gifted men who are 'apt to teach' and who are accepted as such, by a discerning membership. Such teachers will be the first to insist that their service is that of exposition of what God has revealed in His Word.

In seeking a fellowship which conforms to these standards, one needs to beware of the modern cults which deny such doctrines of Scripture as:

(a) The Fall of Man (original sin).
(b) Christ's atoning death.
(c) Christ the one Mediator between God and man.
(d) Christ's essential Deity.
(e) The Person and work of the Holy Spirit.
(f) The Divine Trinity.
(g) Salvation by faith in Christ alone.
(h) The inerrancy of Holy Scripture, as given.
(i) The Second Coming of Christ, for, and with, His Church, and to establish His Kingdom.

These are some of the essential doctrines of Scripture which must be accepted before one can qualify or become a member of the local church as it is described in the Word. The only complete number is contained in the Scriptures, but generally the above mentioned are denied by the modern cults, and in some respects by the historic churches and the World Council of Churches, with its latitudinarian disregard of doctrinal essentials for faith and practice. In spite of its plausible arguments supported by isolated texts wrested from their context. Any member church should be avoided.

Perfection must not be taken for granted in any one church, but credit must be given to one which is making every endeavour to return to the simplicity of the early church at Pentecost. As Mr George Goodman once remarked, such can say in all honesty, 'We do not claim to be the Lord's army, but seek to occupy the ground where the army should stand.'

Naturally differences of interpretation must be allowed on minor points, but insistence on the acceptance of fundamental truth is imperative.

The local church may be small or large, as the Saviour said, 'where two or three are gathered together in my name, there am I in the midst of them' (Matthew 18:20).

The reader may ask, 'Can this be proven as a viable principle in modern church life? The answer is an emphatic 'Yes'. It has been proved in all ages that when one is exercised to found a local church (or assembly) with nothing more than God's Word as his guide, the Lord will bring together others of like mind to achieve His purpose.

One of the most striking examples of this in recent years is to be found in the Communist world where there is no encouragement whatsoever to establish Christian gatherings. We recently attended a missionary gathering in Cornwall where a native Angolan medical student was invited at short notice to report on the Christian church in that country. He stated that in recent years two thousand churches had been started from scratch with no buildings, no funds, and very few experienced teachers; but they had the Scriptures (in limited numbers!) to guide them. So responsive were those that heard the message of salvation, that they were coming in their thousands to Christ, and in one brief period one thousand candidates were baptised by immersion, as a confession of their faith. This young man was an inspiration to all those present, and evidenced a radiant joy coupled with firm convictions, and a maturity which put the British believers to shame. How true are the Lord's words, 'Go out into the highways and hedges, and compel *them* to come in, that my house may be filled' (Luke 14:23).

Quoting once more from William Lincoln, who wrote during the early years of the present century:

'The true church of God is awaking up, as Eve, to the blessed consciousness of her own corporate existence, and of His love as her heavenly Bridegroom, and of the glory awaiting her when He comes, so too now in an unprecedented manner; and in hundreds of places in this and other lands, is the loved church beginning to own and to act on the attraction found in the one Name, and to be assembled solely unto it as the true church ground, according to Matthew 18; and by that very action separating herself in His mystic body and bride from all defilement, and from the dead religious souls all around her, unto Him who Himself is also raised from the dead ones by the glory of the Father...

> Even now from many of these true
> assemblies of His people, the cry is
> beginning to be heard; not her own cry, as
> of the Bride only, but of the Spirit Himself
> within her, yea, cojointly—'the Spirit and
> the Bride say, Come'.' *Typical Foreshadowings
> in Genesis* (pp.212-213).

We hold it as a scriptural principle that the local
church is autonomous, humanly speaking, having
all the gifts within itself for its harmonious
functioning. This cannot be said of any denominational branch of Christendom, nor of the
cults, and certainly not any body embraced by the
World Council of Churches.

The misguided use of the scriptural terms
'bishop', 'pastor', 'evangelist', and 'teacher' will have
little meaning for one who seeks an understanding
from the Scriptures for the operation of these gifts
under the Spirit's guidance.

Being autonomous the church will formulate its
own modes of worship and service, being guided by
Scripture and the operation of the Holy Spirit;
which church hopefully will recognise those qualified
to render such services, and encourage their
exercise. Each church will be entirely independent
of other churches, with no overall governing body,
though when several such churches are impelled by
a similar motive it would be strange if there were no
interchange of fellowship, and offers of mutual
help. This would be the full expression of indepen-
dence and healthy fellowship.

Dr F A Tatford, dealing with problems facing
humanity in the days in which we live, in his book

Five Minutes to Midnight (p.62) expresses ideas very much in harmony with the foregoing:

> 'In the light of the prophetic word, it is difficult to see how any christian can have any part in the building of a united church under the headship of Rome, incorporating conflicting loyalties and beliefs, composed of modernists and evangelicals, and regenerate and unregenerate and even extending a cloak over religions which do not acknowledge Christ at all. The unity of the true church is not organisational but spiritual, created and maintained by the Holy Spirit, and appropriate only to those who are members of the one body, by faith in Christ and His atoning work. Any other unity is of human construction and not of divine origin. The Babylonian harlot produced by man's effort will be destroyed by the physical power which she supported and dominated, but nothing can shake the fabric of the true church, and even "the gates of hell shall not prevail against it" (Matthew 16:18). If the formation of the false church seems to be on the horizon, then the return of Christ for the true church cannot be long postponed.'

A final word of encouragement from the Master Himself, 'Who then is that faithful and wise steward whom *His* Lord shall make *ruler* over His household, to give *them their* portion of meat in due season. Blessed is that servant, whom his lord when

He cometh shall find so doing' (Luke 12:42).

'And let us not be weary in well doing: for in due season, we shall reap if we faint not' (Galatians 6:9).

The greatest reward of all will surely be His, 'Well done'!

Appendix 'A'

DANIEL'S 70 WEEKS OF PROPHECY

(Daniel 9:24-27)

As much of the foregoing is concerned with prophecies relating to Israel, we are reproducing a chart, which was compiled by the late Sir Edward Denny with his own comments and those of 'W.S.' (Walter Scott, author of *The Exposition of the Revelation of Jesus Christ*) and a facsimile copy of Thomas Newberry's comments on the same passage, taken from the Oxford *Englishman's Bible*, bearing his name.

These three well known prophetic writers are agreed as to the interpretation of the prophecy, in contrast with the many unproven theories and unreliable dates which have been deduced by writers over the centuries.

The only dates the passage requires for its understanding is that of the Crucifixion, which is known to have occurred during the Spring of AD 29 (allowing for the 4 year error in the calendar which has been corrected as a result of historically and astronomically proven dates). The crucifixion occurred at the end of the first 483 years of Daniel's prophecy. He wrote during the first year of Darius' reign (about 538BC) and the decree mentioned by Daniel was made by the Persian King Artaxerxes for the rebuilding of the streets and walls of

Jerusalem 'about 445BC', (Nehemiah 2); which date is confirmed by the chart to have occurred 483 years before the crucifixion.

Although these proofs are of interest, we hold that when God speaks, faith accepts His messages without any such need.

In view of the world situation, political, national and in the field of religion itself, we believe there is every indication that the last seven traumatic years of Daniel's prophecy yet to be completed, are nigh at hand. Their importance is stressed by the fact that the archangel Gabriel, who in all four of his recorded appearances, is associated with Israel (see Daniel 8:13-27, 9:21; Luke 1:11-19, 26-33) was sent by the Lord Himself to make known His purposes.

Note

THE SEVENTY WEEKS OF DANIEL

Daniel 9:24-27

'Seventy weeks[1] [*of years, in contrast with weeks of days,* Dan. 10:2, *margin*] are determined [*lit. cut out or divided*] upon thy people, [*Daniel's people, Israel*] and upon thy holy city, [*Jerusalem,* Matt. 27:53; Rev. 11:2] ...

Know therefore and understand, that from the going forth of the commandment to restore and to build Jerusalem [*see* Neh. 2, *about BC446; the safest plan is to reckon backwards*] unto Messiah the Prince [*unto His coming as Prince of Peace to establish His Kingdom: in all seventy weeks, thus cut out or divided:*] shall be seven weeks:[2] [*during this period*] the street shall be built again, and the wall, even in troublous times [*see* Neh.]: and threescore and two weeks. And after the [*Heb.* ha] threescore and two weeks[3] [*these with the seven weeks mentioned before make sixty-nine weeks*] shall Messiah be cut off, but not for Himself; [*the Crucifixion was AD33, but as AD begins four years after the birth of Christ, four years must be added. From the Crucifixion till Antichrist, time is not reckoned, because during this period Israel is not regarded as God's people, nor Jerusalem as the holy city: thus the seventieth week is cut off or divided from the*

[1] 70 weeks = 490 years.
[2] 7 weeks = 49 years.
[3] 62 weeks = 434 years.

199

previous sixty-nine weeks of years] and the people [*the Roman people*] of the prince that shall come [*Antichrist*] shall destroy the city and the sanctuary; [*under Titus, AD70*] and unto the end of the war desolations are determined.

And he [*Antichrist*] shall confirm a [*not* the] covenant with many for one week:[1] and in the midst of the week shall he cause the sacrifice and oblation to cease, [*Antichrist breaks the covenant in the midst, thus dividing the week into two halves; during the first half-week the two Witnesses prophesy, during the last half-week is the Great Tribulation*] and for the overspreading of abominations he shall make it desolate, even until the consummation, and that determined shall be poured upon the desolate' [*or* desolator, (Luke 21:24; Rev. 21:19-21)].

Chart by the late Sir Edward Denny, Bart.

To whom does the prophecy of the seventy weeks refer—to Christians or Jews? To the latter undoubtedly. Daniel's people and city, that is, the Jews and Jerusalem, are the subjects of the prophecy. The futurity of the 70th week, and the latter half of it variously spoken of as 42 months; 1260 days; time, times and half a time, and which cover that solemn period referred to in the central part of the Apocalypse—are profoundly interesting, and absolutely needful to know if the prophecies are to be scripturally apprehended.

Are the weeks periods of days or years? All competent Hebraists hold that the "week" simply

[1] 1 week = 7 years.

denotes "seven"—of days, years, or periods, must be learned from the context; the word itself does not determine. Says the learned Tregelles: "I retain the word 'week' for convenience sake, and not as implying seven days to be the import of the Hebrew word." That they are weeks of years is evident on the surface of the prophecy. But another important inquiry meets us. When did the 70 weeks or 490 years commence? We are informed that it was "from the going forth of the commandment to restore and to build *Jerusalem.*" Now, in the books of Ezra and Nehemiah, we meet with several decrees, but only *one* in reference to the building of Jerusalem; the others refer to the *Temple.* This special commandment or decree, therefore, will be found recorded in the last historical book of the Old Testament—Nehemiah, chapter 2.

The whole duration of the prophecy is divided into three parts:

(1) Seven weeks or 49 years;
(2) Sixty-two weeks or 434 years;
(3) One week or seven years.

Why are they thus separated? Because we have three great events connected with these periods. The rebuilding of the city occupied 49 years; then, from the rebuilding of the city till the coming of Messiah, 434 years; then follow—to complete the whole number—seven years, in which the Prince of the Roman people will league himself with the unbelieving and apostate part of the nation. Observe, very carefully, that *"after"* the building of the city, and *"after"* Messiah had come and presented Himself to Israel, according to Zech. 9:9, which

compare with Matt. 21:5—a period of 483 years
—certain events come in *before* the 70th week
begins.

What are these events? They are plainly noted in
verse 26, Dan. 9; Messiah cut off; Jerusalem
destroyed by the Romans, and a time of desolation
"determined" upon the city and people. The course,
then, of the 70 weeks was interrupted by certain
events happening between the 69th and the 70th.
The whole ran on consecutively till the 69th had
run its course, then comes a break, in which,
amongst other things, a lengthened period of
desolation is determined upon Judaea. During this
long and present desolation upon God's ancient
people, the church is being called out. Israel has
been judicially set aside as God's witness on the
earth, and the Gentile now called in to occupy
Israel's place of public testimony (Rom. 11). When
the church is gathered, Christ will come from
Heaven and take her to Himself, then to the
Father's house, and on to His kingdom and glory.
Thus the long break between these last weeks is
doubly characterised: (1) by Jerusalem's desolation
still going on, the subject of prophetic testimony; (2)
by the calling out of the church, also *going on*, the
subject of apostolic ministry. When the interval
closes, the 70th week, or closing seven years, will
commence with the Prince (whose people, the
Romans, destroyed Jerusalem in the year 70)
making an alliance with the apostate nation then
restored to the land and owning the Antichrist as
prophet and king. The relation of this future week
to the revived Roman empire in its ten-kingdom

form, and to Christendom and Judaism, is unfolded
from chapters 6 to 19 of the Apocalypse.

W.S.

Appendix 'B'

The allotments of Benjamin, Judah and 'the prince' in the Millennium

The map of Palestine reproduced here, together with the enlarged insert of the Temple area, with the Priests' and Levites' prescribed areas, is intended to assist the reader to understand the relationship of Judah and Benjamin to the prince's inheritance and the remaining ten tribes, during the Millennium reign of Christ. Judah and Benjamin having suffered heavily during the Great Tribulation are assigned a position of nearness to the city of Jerusalem and Temple as the saved remnant of the nation of Israel.

The sketches are copied from John Ashton Savage's 'Scroll of Time' a standard prophetic work, with the writer's own explanation of them reproduced in facsimile.

The reference to 'the prince' in the last paragraph is thought by some to refer to Christ, but this does not seem to be a satisfactory interpretation; he is never spoken of in terms of Deity; he personally offers sacrifices and is implied to be a family man with children and servants, (Ezekiel 34:23-24; 37:24-25; 46:15-18 and Hosea 3:3-5).

In the absence of the more satisfactory interpretation these scriptures seem to admit of the possibility that David, who will be resurrected at the coming of the Lord, will act as Viceregent to the

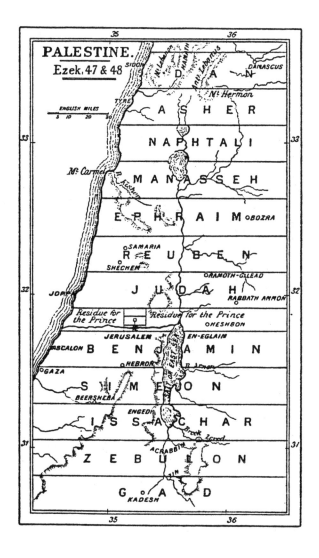

Lord in the Kingdom, which would not conflict with any Old Testament prophecies.

When the Israelites shall have come into full possession of their land, it will be divided among them in accordance with the original and divine purpose of God, as announced in Deuteronomy 32:8,9—"When the most High divided to the nations their inheritance, when he separated the sons of Adam, he set the bounds of the people according to the number of the children of Israel. For the Lord's portion is his people; Jacob is the lot of his inheritance." The whole of Palestine, from the river of Egypt (the Nile) to the great river Euphrates, will be distributed among the restored twelve tribes of Israel on a systematic plan, according to special directions given by God Himself; of which we have a full account in Ezekiel 47 and 48. From these chapters we learn that the land will be divided into twelve parallel segments, running from east to west. (See the Map of Palestine.)

In addition to these twelve divisions, a square portion is to be offered as an holy oblation to the Lord between the allotments of Judah and Benjamin. "All the oblation shall be five and twenty thousand by five and twenty thousand: ye shall offer the holy oblation foursquare, with the possession of the city" (Ezek. 48:20). "And the sanctuary shall be in the midst of it" (v.8). Assuming these measurements to be in cubits (of twenty-one inches to the cubit), it will be a little over eight miles square. It is to be divided into three parallel portions; two of the same size, and the third smaller. The first (the *central* and most important) is the "holy portion," twenty-five thousand (cubits) in length by ten thousand in breadth. "In it shall be the sanctuary *and* the most holy *place*. The holy *portion* of the land shall be for the priests, the ministers of the sanctuary, which shall come near to minister unto the Lord" (Ezek. 45:3, 4).

The second, on the *north* side of the square, is also to be ten thousand in breadth; and shall be for "the Levites, the ministers of the house" (v.5). The third or smaller portion on the *south* side shall be the same length as the first two, but only five thousand broad; for a "possession of the city" (Jerusalem). It "shall be a profane *place* for the city, for dwelling, and for suburbs; and the city shall be in the midst thereof" (Ezekiel 48:15).

The remaining portions on either side of the whole oblation, east and west, shall be for the prince for his possession: "And the residue *shall be* for the prince, on the one side and on the other of the holy oblation" (Ezek. 48:21). "In the land shall be his possession in Israel: and my princes shall no more oppress my people; *and the rest* of the land shall they give to the house of Israel according to their tribes" (Ezek. 45:8). (See Map and Diagram.)

JUDAH.

THE HOLY OBLATION.

25,000 cubits in length.

Residue for the PRINCE.	25,000 cubits in breadth.	Holy portion for the LEVITES.	10,000	Residue for the PRINCE.
		Sanctuary.	10,000	
		□		
		Most holy portion for the PRIESTS.		
River.		Common	City	Place.	5,000	River.

BENJAMIN.

The sanctuary is to be exactly in the midst of the Holy Square, and in the centre of the priests' portion from east to west, but a little to the north of that portion, so as to be in the middle of the whole.

Appendix 'C'

THE ECUMENICAL MOVEMENT — IS IT OF GOD?

Before any attempt is made to answer this question, we must first examine briefly how, and why, the Ecumenical Movement came into being.

From the time of the founding of the church at Pentecost, before the canon of Scripture was compiled, by the addition of the New Testament writings, the Apostles of the Lord and St. Paul were the Divinely appointed authority for the functioning and guidance of the early church. We read that 'the believers continued steadfastly in the apostles' doctrine' (Acts 2:44 AV).

This practice obtained until the twelve Apostles passed away, and the 'early Fathers' succeeded them. Paul had already warned the church at Ephesus, 'after my departure shall grievous wolves enter in among you, not sparing the flock. Also of your own selves shall men arise, speaking perverse things to draw away disciples after them' (Acts 20:29-30 AV).

It required but one generation of the early Fathers to pervert the Apostles' doctrine. For example, Ignatius, a disciple of the apostle John, wrote to the Magnesians saying:

> 'I exhort you that ye study to do all things in a Divine concord, *your bishops presiding in the place of God.*'

It was in the early centuries that the first divisions occurred in the church. A faction consisting the Armenian, Nestorian, Jacobite and Coptic churches taught a heresy involving the relationship of Christ to God and man. These were eventually excommunicated by the Council of Chalcedon (AD451), leaving as a legacy the prototype of the unitarian cults of today. These, with the possible exception of the Unitarians themselves, are not at present interested in the Ecumenical Movement.

During this period the Emperor Constantine (AD274-338) made a profession of faith in Christ, and issued a decree ordering that Christianity was to become the official religion of the Roman Empire. The Emperor saw the church as a force which could enhance his own prestige and authority. To implement his decree he saw the need for an authority within the church which would be answerable to himself. For this purpose prominent men in the church were segregated to create a priesthood. This *third order* of ministry was an addition to the priesthood of all believers, and the Great High the Priesthood of Christ, which had hitherto been recognised as the scriptural position. As a result a distinction was drawn between the humanly ordained priesthood and the laity, which is a feature of the vast majority of the Christian denominations of today. That it is nothing more than a tradition is acknowledged by the Ecumenical movement:

> 'appeal to the text of the New Testament or to the history of the apostolic age has failed to establish a form of ministry

which corresponds precisely to that of
any of the modern churches.'
C of E Response to BEM and ARCIC 1985
para 89 (See Note).

The one outstanding fact which needs to be
recognised, is that the separation which began with
Constantine has subsisted until the present time,
and in spite of all the divisions which have occurred
in Christendom during the intervening years the
wrong which was done has not been recognised by
them, nor has there been a broadly based desire to
return to scriptural principles, as a solution to
denominational divisions.

It has been estimated that, worldwide, there are
at present some 180 Christian denominations,
which, in itself, indicates the extent, and also the
futility, of the problem facing the Ecumenical
movement. The majority of these are numerically
small, leaving the main historic churches to form
the hard core of the movement. These have
abandoned any idea of unity based on the New
Testament pattern; their aim is merely to com-
promise on practices which already exist among
them, whether scriptural or otherwise. The following chart traces the main stream from the apostolic
period, and the various schisms and divisions which
make up the Ecumenical movement of today.

Main Church Groupings from the Apostolic Period

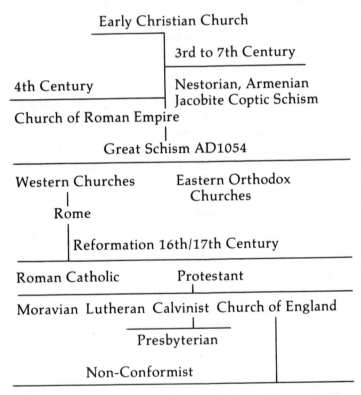

Early Christian Church

3rd to 7th Century

4th Century

Nestorian, Armenian
Jacobite Coptic Schism

Church of Roman Empire

Great Schism AD1054

Western Churches   Eastern Orthodox
                            Churches

Rome

Reformation 16th/17th Century

Roman Catholic   Protestant

Moravian Lutheran Calvinist Church of England

Presbyterian

Non-Conformist

Baptist   Congregational Methodist Evangelical
              Modernist   Anglo-Catholic

II

Faced with such an admixture of professing churches, it obviously became clear to the aspirants of 'church unity' that it would be well nigh impossible to discover any mutual ground for unity among themselves except on the basis of common practices or traditions, especially as a resort to the authority of Scripture was never uppermost in the thinking of the majority.

There had been expressed at the World Missionary Conference held in Edinburgh as early as the year 1910, that some body needed to be formed to unite the churches of Christendom.

Eventually the World Council of Churches emerged in 1927 as a direct result of that Conference, initially with the formation of the 'Faith and Order Commission'. An abortive attempt had been made to achieve some measure of unity among Evangelicals in 1973 by the United Evangelical Congress at Church House, Westminster, during the month of June 1923, with the basic idea that 'differences of outlook and conviction were of secondary importance, so long as the men are loyal to the gospel of Salvation through our Lord Jesus Christ.'

> Preface to the Report on the Conference Addresses on Christian Unity, and the Gospel.
> H. and S.

It is instructive to note from a reading of these addresses that of the 18 given to promote this end only about five of the speakers based their proposals on a clear understanding of the difference between 'church unity' and 'the unity of the Spirit' which may be defined as 'oneness according to the Word of God.'

The five who seemed to understand the distinction were E.L. Langston, I. Siviter, Frederick C. Spurr, W.Y. Fullerton and the Honorable W. Talbot Rice; the remainder appeared to be thinking along the lines of the World Council of Churches as it later emerged.

When it was formed in 1927 the Faith and Order Commission at Lausanne discussed 'Baptism, Eucharist and Ministry', which were deemed to be the main areas of Christian belief and practice. These discussions were continued until 1974, when they reached their present stage of finality at the 'Accra' Talks.

The mature Lima test (BEM) of 1982 has become the basis of interchurch and local discussion today.

In the year 1970, parallel with the W.C.C. (B.E.M.) discussions another important development began to take shape in the form of 'The Anglican-Roman Catholic International Commission' (ARCIC) in its search for a basis for union.

Except for the sending of 'observers' the Roman Church had not hitherto been involved in Ecumenical discussions. It then needed but one year for the Commission to produce the 'Windsor' statement on Eucharist doctrine in 1971. This was followed by the Canterbury statement on Ministry and Ordination in 1973, and was welcomed by the General Synod of the Anglican Church in November 1974. This commended it for acceptance at parochial level in the interests of 'Church unity'. Finally in 1985 an advisory group of 15 Anglicans, chaired by the Bishop of Chichester, with the addition of a consultant and three observers, published a Report on behalf of the Board for Missions and Unity of the General Synod of the Church of England (The Response of 1985).

Having been produced by the highest authorities in the Churches, and passed by Synod it invited opinion at parochial level for its favourable implementation; however, this may prove the most difficult hurdle to surmount.

The 'Response' recognises the problem of presenting a report 'couched in language familiar to theologians which can be popularised and disseminated' (para 163): These Reports are not for the average member in the pew!

III

To consider the Lima (BEM) text the standard required is very simply, 'Does it conform to the New Testament teaching or is it the sum total of traditions which have aggregated over many centuries, and which the churches of Christendom are seeking to reconcile by the joint processes of absorption and concession, in order to reach a consensus of opinion which will prove acceptable to the churches involved?

Regrettably the answer is that though there are certain statements which claim a Biblical basis for the BEM proposals, these are offset by the advocacy of practices which can only be regarded as a denial of Scriptural authority.

Baptism

In the matter of the mode and purposes of Baptism by water we can agree that it is a confession of the candidate's identification with Christ in His death and resurrection, but the essential element of faith in Christ as a precurser to this act of obedience is not clearly stated (para 33). Instead baptism is claimed to be a 'washing away of sin, a new birth ..., an act of justification', and many other features which cannot be attributed to baptism.

Nothing could be clearer than Peter's statement, using the type of the deluge on Noah's day, 'wherein few, that is, eight souls were saved *through water; which also after a true likeness doth now save us, even* baptism, *not the putting away of the filth of the flesh, but the interrogation of a good conscience toward God,* through the resurrection of Christ' (1 Peter 3:20-21 RV). As to the mode of baptism, Peter's insistence of 'a good conscience' eliminates infant sprinkling on the part of those whose conscience cannot be exercised in the matter!

Conybeare and Howson in 'Life and Letters of St. Paul', admit in a footnote to their comments of Romans ch. 6 that at the first the mode of baptism was by immersion. But for lack of space, much more could be written on this subject.

Eucharist

In the same way an examination of the subject of
Eucharist (paras. 56-80), reveals an accretion of
dogmas and practices which by no stretch of
imagination can be supported by a reference to
Scripture. The clearest Biblical statements concerning the purpose of the Lord's Supper are based on
the idea that the celebration is one of 'remembrance'
linking it with a past event in the mind of the
worshipper, an event never needing to be repeated.
As the writer to the Hebrews states, 'we have been
sanctified through the offering of the body of Jesus
Christ once for all' (Hebrews 10:10 RV).

'The paragraphs 58-63 give a fair presentation of
the traditional Anglican attitude to the Lord's
Supper, with which few evangelical believers would
disagree. That the feast is an 'Anamnesis' (remembrance) only, is acknowledged in the BEM report
quoted by the above paragraphs.

The Final Report of ARCIC however states,
'Communion with Christ in the eucharist, pre-
supposes his true presence effectively signified by
the bread and wine which, in this mystery, become
the body and blood.' (para 71).

The three definitive statements in the New
Testament making use of the word ANAMNESIS,
in each instance rendered 'remembrance', are as
follows:

> 'And he took bread, and when he had
> given thanks, he brake it, and gave it to
> them, saying, "This is my body which is
> given for you; this do in *remembrance* of me.

And the cup in like manner after supper, saying, "This cup is the new covenant in my blood, even that is poured out for you" ' (Luke 22:19-20 RV).

'The Lord Jesus in the night in which he was betrayed took bread; And when he had given thanks, he brake it and said, This is my body, which is for you, this do in *remembrance* of me.

In like manner also the cup, after supper, saying, This cup is the new testament in my blood; this do, as oft as ye drink *it*, in *remembrance* of me. For as often as ye eat this bread, and drink the cup, ye proclaim the Lord's death till He come' 1 Corinthians 11:23-26 RV.

Quoting Mr. W.E. Vine's comment from his *Expository Dictionary of New Testament Words*, he writes:

'ANAMNESIS is used (a) in Christ's command in the institution of the Lord's Supper. (Luke 22:19; 1 Corinthians 11:24-25) not in memory of, but in an affectionate calling of the Person Himself to mind.' p.946-7.

In these quotations from Scripture relating in time, to both before the crucifixion, and after it, we cannot conceive of one meaning being different in character from the other so far as the 'real presence' claim is concerned. When our Lord instituted the feast of remembrance it was to be a pattern for the Church from its founding at Pentecost, 'until He come'. The pattern given by the Lord Himself could not be different in character from that described in

Corinthians. If therefore the bread and wine used in the upper room was so plainly symbolic, since the Lord was present in flesh, it must be stressed that the emblems of today's Lord's Supper are equally representative only.

One must agree with Bonar's hymn:—

Only bread and only wine
But to faith the solemn sign
Of the heavenly and divine
We give Thee thanks, O Lord.

The phrase 'Lord's Supper' in both *Vine's Dictionary* and *Young's Concordance* is shown using the term 'Lord's' as an adjective; in other words the emphasis is directed to the Person, rather than to the elements of the Supper. By contrast the doctrine of transubstantiation adds an unwarranted value to the bread and wine. This becomes the more objectionable when they are reserved for administration to the sick and dying with its risk of giving the recipient a sense of false security.

The changes being foisted on many unsuspecting church members after hundreds of years of sound doctrinal teaching on the Lord's supper is regrettable in the extreme.

Ministry

When one examines the reasons put forward for the universal acceptance of the assumed 'third order' of priesthood, in other words, the ordained ministry, there is the clearest indication that the scriptures refuse to support any such structure. There is a difference between the ordained priesthood which assumes *authority over* the local church, or a group of churches, and, in the last resort, 'the universal church', and the case of the local church which is *guided* by elders whose ministry is confined to their own company only. The distinction is clearly that the one rules according to the Canon law of the Church, and the other **serves** according to the principles laid down in the New Testament scriptures. (In the Ecumenical context the aim is toward one universal Canon law).

Peter wrote as follows:

> 'The elders therefore among you I exhort, who am a fellow-elder ... Tend the flock of God which is among you, exercising the oversight, not of constraint but willingly according unto God; nor yet for filthy lucre, but of a ready mind. Neither as *lording* it over the charge allotted to you, but making yourselves ensamples to the flock' (1 Peter 5:1-3 RV).

This passage makes it quite clear that Peter made no claim to authority except in the sense that as an apostle, he among the rest of the Apostles, constituted the foundation of the spiritual church of God, and as such gave guidelines for the churches which would survive the apostle's age. Paul described the relationship of the church to the apostles thus:

> 'ye are fellow-citizens with the saints, and of the household of God. Being built upon the foundation of the apostles and pro-phets' (Ephesians 2:19-20 RV).

With the death of the apostles that authority died

with them!

We are therefore assured that the 'third order of priests', as it is termed in the 'Response' Report is a fabrication, and the final test of a man's position in the church in God's sight is simply whether he *rules* or *serves*. (1 Peter 5:3).

The ARCIC Report makes it quite clear that the ordained ministry as it is headed up in its bishops, and higher dignitaries, has authority over every member in every church within its orbit for discipline. Local responsibility on the part of the recognised elders is over-ridden.

The end result of this distortion of truth, which claims that all men holding the offices implied are the successor to the apostles, is that the difficulties facing the church today are to a very large extent the result of the 'third order' of priesthood. If there were no humanly ordained priesthood the question of women's ordination could never arise! The assumed right to supervise at the Lord's Supper, to conduct baptisms of any kind, and to exercise all the claims which this order makes for itself, would cease to operate when once the scriptural order for ministry is observed.

We therefore conclude that the claim made so strenuously by the Ecumenical Movement that it is 'a great movement of the Spirit' is entirely a false assumption. It is inconceivable that a movement which destroys the harmony between the written Word of God and the workings of the Spirit can be of God.

The answer to the question, heading this Appendix, is therefore an emphatic 'No'.

It seems unnecessary to take up more of the reader's time by any consideration of the Final Report (ARCIC) of the Anglo-Roman Catholic International Commission. The views expressed, about the third order of priesthood in the BEM report, and the insistence on the authority of Scripture, with its teaching on the autonomy of the local church, answers every question which can be raised. The only question remaining for any believer, exercised about what his or her response is to be when the truth of what has been stated is understood, is largely a matter for the individual to decide.

Certainly any church seeking to further the Ecumenical aims and objectives should be avoided, and the nearer one can move toward the autonomous church should be preferred. The Lord may be relied upon to guide in this matter, as He said, 'If any man will to do His will, he shall know of the doctrine, whether it be of God, or *whether* I speak of myself' (John 7:17 AV).

There is every indication that a final agreement on 'church unity' among all parties is not far from realisation. The Final Lima Report which forms the basis of agreement outside the Roman Church is seen by the members of the Anglican faith and Order Advisory Group as a satisfactory instrument for unity. To quote from the 1985 'Response' Summary (p.105) it (the Group) further believes that the theological convergence of this W.C.C. Lima text is not contradicted by the agreement of the Final Report of the Anglo-Roman Catholic International Commission (p.105 para 266). Agreement seems sufficiently near for the Advisory Group to suggest that a symbolic act similar to that of Pope Paul II's visit to Canterbury in 1983, with the remaking of baptismal vows, or the Lutheran celebration in Germany, also in 1983, is desirable.

'Some appropriate celebration might take place in England within the context of the new initiative of the British Churches on the nature and purpose of the Church. Internationally the occasion of the World Conference on Faith and Order in 1989 in Lausanne might provide an opportunity to celebrate the theological convergence on a wider scale' (para 148).

'These are challenging times! Bold decisions on the part of every true believer are called for. We leave the final word with Mr. W.E. Vine from his booklet 'The Origin and Rise of Ecclesiasticism and the Papal System' (p.47).

'The Faith which has been "once for all delivered to the saints" is a complete cycle of Divine Instruction. It claims the obedience of those who would do the will of God. Only by faithfully fulfilling that which is therein revealed can we do what is pleasing to God, meet with His entire approbation here, and receive our full reward hereafter. Those who have shaken themselves free from the shackles of ecclesiastical tradition in whatever shape or form, and have followed the light of truth as taught by Christ and the Apostles have found therein complete satisfaction for the soul and a joyous consciousness of the fulfilment of the will of God.

These are days of confusion. There is a call to

escape from the bonds of materialism, from even the remnants of clerical contravention of the Word of God concerning Church truth, and to recognise the guidance and prerogatives of the Spirit of God and the spiritual ministry which He provides.

Our future and eternal rewards for faithfulness to God will depend upon our adherence simply and solely to the Scriptures.'